A Letter to Young Black Men
You Won't Find Role Models on Street Corners

Eliot Battle

A Letter to Young Black Men
You Won't Find Role Models On Street Corners

Eliot F. Battle

Tucker Publications, Inc.
Lisle, Illinois

TUCKER PUBLICATIONS, INC.
Post Office Box 580
Lisle, Illinois 60532-0580

Serving Minority Publishing Needs Since 1988

Copyright © 1997 Eliot F. Battle

All rights reserved. No part of this book may be reproduced in any form or by any electronic or mechanical means, including information storage and retrieval systems, without permission in writing from the publisher, except by a reviewer who may quote brief passages in a review.

Library of Congress Catalog Card Number 97-061435

Battle, Eliot F.
A Letter to Young Black Men: You Won't Find Role Models on Street Corners

ISBN   0-923950-18-4

Typeset by Distinctive Designs, Batavia, IL
Printed & bound by Columbus Bookbinders & Printers, Columbus, GA
Cover design by Jillian Kingsford Smith, Columbia, MO

Printed in the United States of America
First Printing: August, 1997 $15.00

Foreword

Eliot F. Battle is a teacher, and like the admonition to the teacher in Kahlil Gibran's *The Prophet*, he seeks to reveal to you, African American youth, "that which already lies half asleep in the dawning of your knowledge." Also, in keeping with the advice to the teacher in *The Prophet*, Mr. Battle "does not bid you enter the house of his wisdom, but rather leads you to the threshold of your own mind."

The message in "A Letter to Young Black Men" is a call to young people of the 1990's to recapture the vision that African American youth have held and nurtured in every generation since the arrival of African people on American shores. We only need to look at fairly recent history to find examples of Black youth following that vision of making the world a better place.

It is fitting that we honor Dr. Martin Luther King, Jr., Malcolm X, Roy Wilkins, A. Philip Randolph, and other leaders of the Civil Rights movement, but we should also remember the young people who had a vision of a better America and who were the real heroes of the movement. In fact, Dr. King was only 26 years old when he became the leader of the Montgomery Bus Boycott. James Farmer was only 21 years old and just out of theology school when he began working to organize CORE as a means of fighting segregation. John Lewis, the son of Alabama farmers and now Congressman John Lewis, was only 15 years old when the Montgomery Bus Boycott began. He was inspired by Dr. King's message and set out to make the world a better place.

Lewis dreamed of attending Dr. King's school, Morehouse College. He could not attend Morehouse, but he was determined to get an education. He entered American Baptist Theological Seminary in Nashville, Tennessee, at 17 and worked in the kitchen to support himself. Lewis became a key figure in the movement as a leader of the Student Nonviolent Coordinating Committee. Julian Bond and Lonnie King were two other young Black men who were both college students at Morehouse and a part of the struggle for equal rights.

Historians of the Civil Rights movement often date the beginnings of the movement from the date that the four young men, who were just a few months out of high school, sat in at the Woolworth's store in Greensboro, North Carolina. These young men did not know that they were role models for many other young Black men. Down in Denmark, South Carolina, 16 year old Cleveland Sellers caught the vision of those Greensboro young men and became a leader of the movement in his hometown.

Many of the participants in the Civil Rights movement of the 1960's and 1970's are leaders in politics, business, and organizations devoted to civic and educational advancement. They are worthy role models for today's young Black men and women. The challenges facing you as young Black men are somewhat different from those which they faced as youth in the 1960's, but meeting today's challenges is just as important to your future and the future of all African Americans as it was for them to meet the challenges they faced.

Mr. Battle is well qualified to speak to you about the road you should follow. He knows the hardships a young Black man had to go through to get an education in his day. He prepared himself for a career in teaching and spent several decades as a teacher, mentor, and role model for young people.

Eliot Battle was born and reared in Mobile, Alabama, during the era of "Jim Crow." The African American community of Mobile was one that formed that "village" that we hear so much about these days that are needed to raise children. The men of his community had high goals and expectations, and they passed these values to the youth. Recognition of the importance of education was high among these values. Equally as high was the work ethic, the realization that nothing worthwhile can be accomplished without hard work. As a young man, Eliot worked at whatever jobs were available, from bus boy to sand-blasting airplane parts.

After high school, he attended Tuskegee Institute, now Tuskegee University, where he helped to meet his college expenses first by cleaning horses and horse stalls. After two years in the stables, he advanced to the more desirable job of guiding visitors around the beautiful Tuskegee campus. At Tuskegee, he was blessed with a great variety of role models, including faculty members, doctors and staff members at the Veteran's Hospital, and visitors to the campus.

Service in the still segregated army at the end of World War II provided him broader experiences and made him even more aware of the importance of education. When he left the army, he returned to Tuskegee and completed a Master's degree. He later earned another Master's degree from the University of Missouri-Columbia.

Mr. Battle had a rich and varied career in education. He began his career as an agriculture teacher of World War II veterans in Poplar Bluff, Missouri. From that position, he moved on to become principal of Dalton Vocational School in Chariton County. When school desegregation led to the closing of this school, he moved to Columbia to become assistant principal and counselor at Douglass School. Then, in 1960, he transferred to Hickman High School, where for four years he was the only African American faculty member. From 1966 until he retired in 1991, he served as Director of Counseling for the Columbia School District. Since retiring from the Columbia Public Schools, Mr. Battle has served as Special Assistant to the President of Columbia College. In all of these positions, he has been a role model and mentor to young people.

The advice and information he shares with you in the pages that follow merit your careful consideration. No group is at greater risk in our society today than our young Black men. The advice in this "Letter" offers a way of lessening that risk.

- Dr. Arvarh E. Strickland
Professor Emeritus of History
University of Missouri - Columbia

Note from the Author

To whom is this book directed?

Our world today offers many and varied opportunities. It seems that the age of technology is boundless in its effects on business and culture. Around the country, we observe new roads, new buildings, high employment levels, and a tremendous depth and variety of educational opportunities.

We blink, we look again, and hidden in the above-described world there is a segment of society which, for many reasons, is not in tune with the whole. There are many young Black men who are at a fork in the road and who may or may not travel the road to productivity and fulfillment. There are those who have already faltered and have made unwise choices. There are young Black men who are at the junior high school level and must be given assistance as they develop their values.

Many young Black men are following paths to success. Many, representing a wide variety of economic levels, follow very positive routes. This group, however, is in constant need of reinforcement.

In answer to the question, "For whom is this book written?" My answer is that it is written for all young Black men, probably ages 12 to adult, as well as for all persons who are striving to understand young Black men. The reading audience could include those young men of households where reading is frequently practiced and who frequent libraries, young Black men who are housed in juvenile centers or homes for delinquent youth, Black churches, Black organizations such as the Links, youth chapters of the NAACP, job centers, those Black men incarcerated in prisons, and leaders who work with young Black men. The main purpose of this book is to say to young Black men that it isn't too late to make a change, and that the comments which we often hear regarding the "lost generation" are not etched in stone.

In "Brothers," a visual portrait of Black men in America written in 1987 by Sylvester Monroe, a Newsweek correspondent, there was a statement alluding to his research: "I thought we might find some answers as to why black men in America seem almost an endangered species."

There is too much violence, too much gang activity, too much "Black on Black" crime. Young Black men need a positive focus. It is the purpose of this book to serve as one ray of hope and to give some young Black men a reason to make positive changes. Some young Black men follow negative paths because they know no other. Every positive role model for these young men serves as a plus. Hopefully, this book will provide some incentive to young Black men to strive for high goals.

— Eliot F. Battle

To My Father

Ralph Waldo Trine in *In Tune with the Infinite*, wrote a passage that eloquently states how my father, the most wonderful role model I know, lives his life:

> *By example and not by precept. By living, not by preaching, By doing, not professing. By living the life, not by dogmatizing as to how it should be lived.*

If you are in need of a consistent role model, please share my father with me. My father is a brilliant teacher but believes we all must also be humble students. My father is a moral, righteous and religious man but never passes judgement on others. My father is a successful, loving and happy man who never forgets how fortunate and blessed he is and never misses an opportunity to pass on his blessings and good fortune. My father is truly a great man who sincerely believes that all men have the potential to be great. My father wrote this book to share his and other successful men's proven formula for success with young men who need a guide for a successful life. From the well worn proven path my father and others have successfully traveled, he graciously shares their thoughts and conclusions on how to approach life and win.

My father's philosophy on how to succeed in life is shared by many successful men. Tecumseh, the proud chief of the Swanee summarized my father's belief when he stated:

> *Love your life, perfect your life, beautify all things in your life. Seek to make your life long and its purpose in the service of your people. Respect others in their view, and demand that they respect yours.*

Read this book and start your journey of success.

I love you dad. Thanks for being persistently and consistently wonderful!

—Eliot F. Battle, Jr., M.D.

Table of Contents

Foreward vii
Note from the Author xi
Note from the Author's Son xii
Table of Contents xiii
Preface xiv
Acknowledgements xvii
Dedication xviii

Chapter   **Page**

1	Introduction	1
2	Young Black Men and Achievement	5
3	Peer Pressure	10
4	Responsibility to Women	13
5	You and Manhood	14
6	Young Black Men and Fatherhood	15
7	No Excuses	17
8	Ingredients for Success	21
9	Ingredients for Failure	26
10	Young Black Men and Conformity	27
11	The Pseudo Leader	29
12	Positive Role Models	30
13	Young Black Male School Dropouts	33
14	Pride	35
15	Goal Setting	37
16	Self Worth	41
17	Purpose	43
18	Character Traits	46
19	Attitude	47
20	Hope	49
21	Decision	51
22	Faith and Decision Making	52
23	Interviews with Outstanding Young Black Men	54
24	Your Obligation as Young Black Men	57
25	Interviews with Incarcerated Young Black Men	60
26	Conclusion: A Personal Challenge to Young Black Men	66

Preface

I am a Black man. I have lived a good life. I have enjoyed all of the things that contribute to happiness. Let me assure you, however, that I wasn't born with a silver spoon in my mouth. My family, like many of yours, struggled to make sure that an education was attained by my brothers, my sisters and me. My parents sacrificed many things in order to provide us with the necessities for life.

As a teenager, in addition to school work, I sold candy and magazines, I worked as a busboy in a hotel restaurant, I worked as a sandblaster at an Air Force base, and as an operator of a blueprint photostat machine for a privately owned business.

During my first year in college, I lived in a private room in the horse barn at Tuskegee University. My job that year was cleaning the stalls and cur-combing and brushing the horses. During my additional years there, I worked as a student guide for visitors to the campus. This was a super experience for me. It afforded me the opportunity to meet, among others, Lena Horne and Joe Louis when they visited Tuskegee.

One of my greatest experiences while a student at Tuskegee was the opportunity to visit with Dr. George Washington Carver, who at that time was working at the Carver Museum. It was exciting to see him at work and to converse with him — a man could study and reach the heights he attained, and yet remain humble.

I am a proud Black man. I am proud of my heritage. I am proud of my personal contributions. I am proud of my wife and children and their personal accomplishments. I am proud of my grandchildren. And I am proud of the many Black men and women whom I have personally watched mature and develop into good and worthwhile people.

I am a Black man who knows what it means to struggle and to persevere. I am hopeful that young Black men will profit from reading this book, and that it will make a difference in their lives.

In 1988, John Jacob, President and CEO of the National Urban League, in an address to the members of the Congressional Clearing House, made the following comment:

> *There is a powerful myth today that the answer to such problems is self-help. That it is the <u>sole</u> responsibility of the black community to eradicate dysfunctional behavior and to pull itself into the mainstream. That's just a myth — without basis in fact or in history... It's all right to talk about pulling yourself up by your bootstraps, but not when you're talking to people who don't have boots.*[4]

I am aware that these comments are still viable. I know that educational and vocational opportunities must be improved at all levels. I am also aware that much effort must be made by each individual at all levels.

Young Black men have a great responsibility. Young men look up to others for their role models. Many young Black men find themselves without the "father" role model, and the Black male teacher is becoming very rare. Even scout leaders are now frequently women. The young Black male has the potential to develop into a quality person, but equally important, also has an opportunity to be someone who is looked up to by younger boys in the neighborhood.

These young men of the neighborhood today see a lot of movies which depict young Black men as hoods or gang members. They read newspaper accounts of negative behaviors of young Black men. They see televised reports of young Black men involved in criminal activity. They know firsthand of some of the crime in their own communities and neighborhoods. They are at the crossroads. They need all the help available. These young Black men are vulnerable. Their parents might help, their ministers, counselors and teachers may assist. You must be one of the older "positive" persons to help them. I realize that this is asking much of you. The changes which all of us want are to eliminate drug and criminal activity and the violence that pervades our neighborhoods.

All of us, in our various challenges, sometimes respond, "But I can't make a difference."

Just think what the world would be if that had been the attitude of those before us. What if our ancestors had concluded, "Why learn to read? We will never be able to use an education." What if Booker T. Washington had not established Tuskegee Institute, or if Dr. Martin Luther King, Jr. had accepted the rules which did not afford opportunities to Black people? What if Thurgood Marshall had been a mediocre attorney and had not been qualified for service on the Supreme Court? What if Michael Jordan or Arthur Ashe had been satisfied with playing basketball or tennis without consistent practice and a determination to win? What if Colin Powell had not allowed education to play a major role in his life? Or if Tiger Woods had said, "Black golfers do not reach the top." These are but a few examples of those Black men who had the attitude, "I can make a difference." You, too, can make a difference.

There are more Black men in prison than there are in college. Each young Black man who determines that he is going to follow a "positive path," not only reduces the number of those incarcerated, but he serves as a role model to many other young Black men, sometimes even unknowingly.

Again, I am aware of the discouragement which some may feel. As young people feel the pangs of discouragement and begin to falter, they must think about those men who would not give up. Think again about Dr. King as he fought for civil rights. He was a man with a mission, and he let no one stop him from reaching his goals. Think again of General Colin Powell. We know that he did not reach the top without some negative critics. Nothing, however, stopped him.

There are, as a result of these men and many others, opportunities for young men in many occupations. Doors are open to young men but only for those who are prepared to obtain and accept new opportunities. You must not sit back and make excuses. Indeed, you must serve as examples to other young men as they continue to accomplish the goals which they have set.

[4] Jacob, John E. (1990, December/1991, January). The future of Black America. *Black Empowerment and Education Journal*, 33-38.

Acknowledgments

There are many Black leaders through the country who responded to my question: **"What advice would you give to young Black men?"** I greatly appreciated their responses and I have used their thoughts as introduction to various segments of the book.

I personally visited with college students, undergraduates and graduates for their views. They were very candid and insightful. It was, however, during interviews with young Black men in prison, that I was given the answer. A young man who was incarcerated for murder said, "Tell them you won't find role models on street corners." I decided to use that statement for my sub-title.

I would like to thank my friend, Dr. Strickland, Professor at the University of Missouri-Columbia. Dr. Strickland, a noted author and the first Black professional at the University of Missouri was very supportive. I know that his words are always an inspiration to young people.

I also acknowledge the good fortune of having grown up in a loving environment with great parents, Charles and Leana Battle, and supportive brothers and sisters Barbara Robinson, Lya Dowe, and Dr. Charles and Dr. Earl Battle.

Dedication

I dedicate this book to my family. My wife Muriel without whose love and encouragement, I would not have written this book. To my four children who all are great achievers and in whom I have much pride. Donna Pierce, Carolyn Thomas, Muriel Jean Browder and Eliot F. Battle, Jr.

A Letter to Young Black Men
You Won't Find Role Models on Street Corners

Chapter 1
Introduction

When I reflect on Dr. Martin Luther King, Jr., and the strength, determination and character which he possessed, I am in awe. I realize that he led a battle for civil rights during a period of strong social resistance. He died for a cause in which he had great belief.

When I look at the many young Black men today who lack determination and who seemingly have little will to achieve, I feel dismay. I know that much change is needed — I feel compelled to write this letter. It is my fervent hope that many Black youth and their support systems will not only read this information but will realize the importance of following its positive suggestions.

As I review the past and recall the limited opportunities that existed for young Black men when I was a youth, I'm encouraged by the current possibilities. When I was a youth, Black men who aspired to enter professional fields were limited generally to teaching, law, medicine, pharmacology, and the ministry. These were the typical and mostly segregated opportunities. Times have changed appreciably. There many more opportunities, and capable Black professionals have a wide variety of choices.

Instead of a lack of opportunity, the problem now, for so many, is a lack of preparation. Having worked in public schools as a guidance director, I have firsthand knowledge of the attitudes of many "cool" young Black men who as adolescents lived for the day and failed to plan for the future. I have talked with many of these young men as adults and have heard the same comment repeatedly, "I wish that I had applied myself earlier."

Taking the easy way out, following the crowd, "playing down" the importance of school and a good fundamental preparation for your future — this approach to living is doing us all a terrible disservice. Most men, as we list the things in life which we most desire, list happiness close to the top. As we list the components of happiness, we include a good family, a comfortable home, a reasonably good income, a job which we enjoy, and good friends. Since these are the things which most men list as being important to happiness and success, why don't young Black men make a meaningful connection, and start early in working toward the goal?

Imagine what it would be like if most young Black men had positive goals and worked diligently toward achieving them. There is no reason that this should be only imagined. Young men could make differences in their lives if they would take a personal inventory and work on improving negative traits.

In the 1930s and 1940s, many Black families seemed to produce successful children. Father, mother, children, and an extended family of aunts, uncles, cousins, and grandparents usually lived in the same communities and were very supportive of each other. A young Black man had many role models. In addition to his parents and relatives, neighbors were a very important factor in providing additional encouragement to young people. There were few television sets, although we did have radios. Automobiles were "family cars" used for necessary transportation and occasionally for pleasure for the extended family. Rarely did young Black men have access to the family car for personal use. There were many family-oriented recreational activities. The main objective of many young people during this period was to secure an education. Most of their activities revolved around school, academics, athletics and being social.

The word most descriptive of Black families and individual members of Black families was "pride." Black people generally took pride in accomplishment and achievement. Possibly, lack of television as well as the relative inaccessibility of automobiles contributed to a high degree of personal determination and achievement. Not only did young Black men take pride in their athletic achievements, they were equally proud of their accomplishments in academics, art, music, public speaking and many other areas.

It was generally understood that a high school diploma was needed to enter the next level of college, vocational training and/or on-the-job training. It was uncommon to hear young Black men referred to as "having little ambition."

World War II, and the years immediately thereafter, brought about many changes. Traveling around the country and changing places of residence became very common. Moving from various army posts or naval bases during the war by service men and their families afforded exposure to new areas of the country as well as new lifestyles. As families moved to new communities, a support system of other relatives and neighbors was no longer common. Role modeling to which young Black men had been exposed declined greatly.

Compounding the developing social problems, the cost of living increased appreciably. Incomes were generally insufficient for adequate family support. Frequently the father was not at home due to working extra hours or two jobs. For the first time, mothers in large numbers also began working outside of the home in order to supplement family incomes. With a new environment away from supportive family members and stable neighbors, and having little supervision by either parent — with this decreased family socialization, young Black men have had difficulty maintaining their values.

The numbers of young Black men in this predicament were great in all major cities. Many large cities were inundated with Black families including teenagers and pre-teenagers with lots of time on their hands. Job opportunities were few. Job training was inaccessible or did not exist. Recreational opportunities were not sufficient. Thousands of young Black men in every major city, many untrained for available employment, played pick-up basketball games and frequently hung out in the neighborhoods, sometimes drinking and/or smoking marijuana.

Further compounding the problem, city planners around the nation employed practices, as a result of their predjudices, which ultimately maintained separatism. Federal laws in the 1940s authorized public housing construction and provided funding nationwide for this purpose. Attempts generally were made to limit Black people to remain in "their" areas.

High rise buildings in some cities, like the failed Pruitt-Igo project in St. Louis, have been razed after years of neglect and deterioration. Pruitt-Igo's debris stood where, fifty years previously, an established Black neighborhood had thrived. It had been the desire of the city fathers, generally, that all of the qualified families for public housing be housed together. With the scarcity of jobs, a forced housing pattern and little family supervision, chaos was the inevitable result.

Instead of general improvements, economic situations worsened. Men struggled to earn a living. Families were forced to go on welfare and accept food stamps. Single mothers were given support for child care. This practice mandated by federal law encouraged the Black males' absence from the home. Teenage boys growing up in the matriarchal home environment began to get a different view of their roles as men in the home. Much of what has happened to the Black male has resulted from public policy.

I wrote the above material so that you would better understand some of the social reasons behind the predicament in which we find ourselves. This, however, does not give us excuses. We must be determined to make a change. This abbreviated account of a major sociological problem is designed to give a pointed overview of a significant problem. Earlier, I made the statement that a term that described Black families was pride. It is my contention that that characteristic has not been lost. I feel that the system has caused a feeling of helplessness among many Black men. When the energy of young Black men is stifled, when instead of being invested in productive work, it is my position that many young Black men hang around in public housing projects, in parks, and on corners, feeling worthless and without opportunities. This situation often breeds anti-social activities, and local jails become these men's temporary homes. Some of these men will become involved in serious offenses and ultimately serve time in state and federal prisons.

Change will come about when young Black men determine that what they experience is not what they want out of life. It is not going to be easy, however, for young men to turn their lives around. They will need support and assistance.

When I pick up newspapers and read about crimes in major cities, I shudder. We are all guilty. We have contributed to the problem as we have allowed our federal, state and local governments to inflict injustice upon a race of people. When we continue to allow a system of forced housing, inadequate schools and double standards of employment practice, problems will persist. We can no longer look the other way and allow people to suffer merely because of their skin color.

Chapter 2
Young Black Men and Achievement

The message I seek to convey to Black males today is one of opportunity. The opportunities available to our young people today, regardless of race, creed, religion or sex, have never been greater. Those who are willing to put forth the effort are dedication and who strive to better themselves through continued education can become whatever they want to be in life. One need not look far to find examples of those who have followed this advice and succeeded – Arthur Ashe, Thurgood Marshall and Reginald Lewis, are but a few of the many examples.

Today's Black males are the next generation of scientists, artists, writers, philosophers, teachers, elected officials, administrators and entertainers. Their dreams are vital to our future, and we must all come to see and know that we can make a difference... and that we make changes, never forgetting from whence we came.

- Lawrence Douglas Wilder
Former Governor, Commonwealth of Virginia

Achievement doesn't come easily. Most worthwhile things don't. Frequently the difference between achievement and failure is attitude. Your ancestors were not acceptors of defeat. Why should young Black men be? A measure of maturity is when we reach for as high a goal as is achievable.

Young Black men have every right to achieve. They must think of themselves and their own future. They must realize that when they decide that they are going to study and achieve, there will be others who will assist them by giving them the courage and strength to redirect their focus. I have witnessed Black students who have not performed adequately because of peer pressure. Other Black students want them to defy the system and not take college-prep courses because this route, they say, is for white students. They must reject this view, and realize that they will regain pride as a result of their own positive performance.

YOU AND AMBITION

During my involvement with public schools, I had the opportunity to see many young Black men become outstanding athletes. Some few combined athletics and academics and went on to successful careers with professional teams. I believe that in order to be an outstanding basketball, baseball, soccer, or football player, a person must have above average intelligence. I have watched many great athletes who very quickly learned and implemented new plays with ease. Many of these young men accepted "C"s and "D"s in school, just barely getting by.

I have no doubt the reason a person is able to become a "star" athlete is due to motivation, determination, and practice. Those same qualities are equally important for academic success. If young men were to show a determined attitude toward school work — study — as determinedly as typical athletes practice, I have no doubt that they would develop "star" quality in academics.

As we look candidly at athletics and the likelihood of a high school athlete becoming a professional one, the chances are somewhat slim. On the other hand, the necessary preparation to achieving goals in college will more than pay for itself in the long run. High achievers can earn scholarships and receive financial assistance for college, including graduate or professional specialty training.

I strongly encourage you to take a personal inventory. Look at where you are and where you would like to be five, then ten years down the road. Review the steps necessary to reach your goals, then start doing the necessary preliminaries.

Obstacles are surmountable. There is no more beautiful sight as that of a high jumper soaring over the extended pole at a top level. It is accomplishment that causes exhilaration on the part of the athlete. The same exhilaration comes when a person breaks a barrier thought not possible, such as when a person achieves a high score on a test for which he has prepared. It's so easy to give up and decide, "Why compete? I won't be able to make a high enough jump to win."

It's also easy to feel that an academic requirement is so high that it's not attainable. Attitude is the key factor in both cases. If a person decides that he cannot accomplish a particular thing, athletic or academic, chances are he will fail. If, on the other hand, a person feels that he can do something, and he practices or studies, achievement becomes more likely.

All young men go through stages of growth and development. It's a natural adolescent phenomenon. Some, however, seem to reach one negative stage and remain there. I call this the "I don't care about anything" stage. One of the most important activities of development is a continuation of positive growth, as opposed to stagnation. When a person allows himself to become stagnant, to level off and stop growing mentally and positively, then he finds himself in a rut. Sometimes young people mistake the wrong people as the enemy. Frequently, parents, teachers, ministers or other responsible adults are mistakenly thought of as the foe, whereas the real enemies to their progress are their assumed friends.

We all take chances. One of the most common money-making techniques used by many of our states is through lotteries. These have millions of dollars for winners. People look at the possible winnings and take chances on the jackpot.

One of the most crucial chances that we take is reaching productive periods in our lives. Odds are much greater for us to become productive, successful adults than winning the lottery. Similarly, students take unnecessary chances — skipping classes or dropping out of school — thinking they can beat the odds. Some think they can make it without study. They practice negative behavioral activities and become "pros" in that arena.

If a person were to redirect his efforts, if he attended all of his classes and participated actively in discussion, spent necessary study time, he would eliminate an element of chance. He would increase the likelihood of above average achievement. If he performs in an above average manner, he will increase his chances of acceptance to a college of his choice. He also will enhance his likelihood of achievement at college as a result of his established study skills.

Some young people think that they are being smart by taking the easy road. Those who do, find the easy road leads to a hard life. Achievers don't take chances with themselves. They set short and long term goals, and keep their eyes on the prize.

What is the difference between the man who achieves and the one who flounders? The achiever decides early in life that he wants to be "somebody." He plans for accomplishment, and he does not follow the crowd. The flounderer seems to go whichever way the wind blows, and does not seem to have a plan or a direction. Persons who are easily led usually end up as non-achievers because they often follow non-motivated leaders. Think about your own friends and acquaintances. Look at those who are squandering their time.

I know that many of you have at some time in your lives participated in team sports of some sort. Team sports differ from individual sports like boxing, track and field, swimming — those activities which call upon you to try to top yourself.

Team sports require an effort from each team member if the group expects to win. The same thing may be said for you in life. Achievement requires individual attainments as well as positive group drive. You will not likely reach positive goals if you only develop individual goals without being part of a group. Nor can you participate with negative groups and expect to reach positive goals. You have to learn to draw the line.

One of the greatest enemies of young people is drugs. They are a special enemy to young Black men who have allowed drugs to become their master. It appears that many young Black men look at cars, jewelry, and material things as evidence of achievement. Young men know that the money spent for these purchases has come through drug related deals. Many young Black men make the unwise choices of following role models from street corners and being led down a bleak path.

Crack cocaine is reported to be a drug used predominantly in Black communities, and the arrests made as a result of drug possession, or of a crime that is drug related, are the most frequently occurring ones.

There's an old saying, "Life is what you make it." Young men have the most critical input into their own future. If they do positive things that involve them in goal-oriented activities, they very likely will have a good life. If, on the other hand, they involve themselves in negative behavior, their future will reflect such choices.

Patience is an outstanding quality. Young men must realize that many of the things they want in life require time to attain. They must learn to take the course slowly and with a good attitude. Most men who achieve do so with patience.

We have all heard the comment, "That young man has high moral character." Just what is meant by that description? High moral character is a quality that is not based on economic or social class. It's instead based upon personal values and how he puts them into practice.

Let me assure you, I don't have my head stuck in the sand. I'm aware of many of the problems which many young Black men have. I know how tough it must be to have obstacles to your goals. Many young Black men do not succumb to obstacles or fall into the trap of negative behavior. As I walk through the halls of colleges and visit young Black men, many first-generation college students, I have great pride. These are students with goals, and they're achieving them very well. When I walk through the halls of prisons and visit these young Black men, my pride turns to sadness and despair. Society has failed. Many of these young men are bright and capable. Most have not had the fortune to have the values instilled in them that are necessary to achieve.

Crime has become a major societal problem which is in need of correction. Many of us are distressed as we pick up newspapers and read of crimes committed by young people nationwide, and the disproportionate number of young Black men. Society does very little to prevent or correct the problems. As I talk with young Black men who are in prison, I get the impression that they're in a no-win situation. A few of the motivated ones prepare for their GED or enroll in college courses, yet the majority appear to simply waste their energy. Many are competent, capable men who could be trained for a productive life. Instead they are obligated to menial, non-inspiring tasks which are of little personal value.

Chapter 3
Peer Pressure

Don't compromise your values. Be true to yourself. In the long run, you will prevail in whatever you attempt.

Sandy Bowers, Former Chief Counsel
Division of Employment Security
State of Missouri

We have all heard the statement, "He made me do it," or "She made me do it." We are all responsible for our own actions. No one can make you do something you don't choose to do. Peer pressure plays a very big part in a teenager's life — what clothes to wear, shoes to buy, friends to make, hours to keep, even what to eat or drink and how to conduct yourself.

Peer pressure is not new. The new phenomenon is the negative peer pressure to which many young Black men have succumbed. Being part of the crowd or in the "in group" is fine as long as the "in group" is involved with positive activities. It would be better to be a part of the "out group" and maintain standards and values. Those who achieve have done just that. Those who practice negative behavior end up in negative settings.

It takes strength not to go along with the masses, but positive strength is contagious. Others want to practice positive conduct but feel somewhat isolated when they do. They will be encouraged to follow your lead. There are many young people who do not enjoy smoking, drinking, or using drugs, but who conform to be part of the crowd. Many young men in prisons around the country are there because of having been influenced by negative peer pressure.

Those young Black men who are conformists no matter how much they disagree with the activities of the leader should be more cautious with their conduct and should realize the negative results of negative behavior. They should also realize that their future depends on the path that they choose now.

I am not suggesting that peer pressure in itself is all bad. Positive peer pressure, which leads persons down roads which help them to become better persons, is very worthwhile. Many people have climbed the road to success with assistance of positive peer pressure.

If someone feels he has made bad choices, let me assure you that it's not too late to change. No man goes through life without making mistakes. When, however, young men continue to make blunders, and these blunders become increasingly serious, then problems are compounded.

Those men who were interviewed in prisons, and discussed in this book, were among thousands nationwide who could have gone either way. They had a tough row to hoe, so to speak, as young boys and men. I don't believe, however, in excuses. It is my contention that each person is responsible for himself and that, with determination, all persons can become successful. Criminal behavior is not natural. It is learned behavior — something which persons adopt. It is a way of avoiding the necessary steps for positive achievement. Thefts and robberies, instead of hard work to accomplish goals, will only lead to self destruction.

I have observed that persons usually achieve in proportion to how they set their sights and how they spend their time deserving their achievements. I strongly believe in the work ethic. I know that job opportunities are fewer than job applicants, however with that realization, it's necessary to be among those job candidates who will be selected for employment. It's so easy to use the excuse, "They didn't hire me because I'm Black." I have no doubt in some instances that's true, but I have no doubt that many Blacks are hired who, in addition to being Black, are competent, dependable, have neat appearances and are confident.

There are many things over which we have no individual control. There are some things, however, which are in our hands. Among the things that we can control are the extent of our schooling, the quality of our school performance, and our moral and ethical behavior, including avoidance of criminal involvement. Let's review a few statistics regarding Blacks in general and their role in the criminal justice system.

Let me share with you some frightening figures from the *1992 F.B.I. Uniform Crime Report* published October 7, 1993. During 1992, there were 19,463 murders and/or non-negligent manslaughters committed. Of these, 8,466 were committed by whites and 10,728 by Blacks. There were 1,162 white and 1,625 Black arrests for this crime committed by persons under 18 years of age. During that same year, 33,332 persons were arrested for forcible rape, of which 18,490 were white and 14,258 were Black; 2,801 were arrests of young white men under 18 years of age and 2,462 were young Black men under 18 years of age.

As you are aware, much of the crime which is committed by Black persons is "Black on Black" crime. As a race we have been, and in many instances continue to be, victimized by others. As this victimizing occurs, the perpetrators should not be excused nor exonerated.

Young men have the power in their hands to correct the F.B.I. reports of the future. They must assume responsibility, and they must appreciably reduce the numbers of Black criminals in every category.

There are thousands of Black men throughout the country who are positive role models. They represent many different professions and occupations. There are many thousands of young Black men who are involved in positive activities who are striving for positive goals. I can only encourage them to continue climbing and to thank them for carrying on the spirit and pride for which our race is known.

If, on the other hand, they have gotten off the positive path, they should endeavor to come back. They owe much to those in the past, and they owe even more to those of the future.

Chapter 4
Responsibility to Women

> *You have it better than your parents did, and hopefully not as well as your children will. Be good to the women in your life. They can be easily hurt by us when we do the wrong and selfish things. Be men, not players.*
>
> Judge Robert Collins

There is something innate in Black men about the respect that they hold for women. For example, the respect that a Black male shows for his mother is one that is very strong. Somehow the societal stresses on Black men have resulted in a change in toward the women in their lives. A part of the macho or gangster image cultivated during the last decade has included the mistreatment of women. I feel that once men regain their own self-respect, the return of attitudes of respect toward women will become automatic.

There are many reasons why this changed attitude is so prevalent. In my opinion, the media, especially television, emphasizes the mistreatment and abuse of women. Many television shows promote violence to women, including mental and/or physical abuse, often with Black men being the perpetrators. Young Black men view and adopt these practices thinking that they are appropriate behaviors. Divorce rates have increased appreciably during the last two decades. Young Black men have witnessed the breakup of the family in large numbers. They have also witnessed abuse and have mistakenly mimicked these practices.

Young Black men must realize the importance of giving respect to Black women. Black women traditionally have been responsible for keeping the family together as a unit. They have worked to see the Black church prosper. They have sacrificed for years to make sure the Black child's wants were few. They deserve to be treated with honor, and it is the Black man who must bestow this honor.

Chapter 5
You and Manhood

What is a man? There is a terrific difference between being a male and being a man. A male is identified anatomically. A man is always, of course, a male, but he is much more than physical characteristics. Many males who are fathers are not truly men.

Manhood encompasses special qualities. Men are responsible and accept their responsibilities. Men possess character. Men have capacity for love which they extend to their children. Men have great amounts of pride and self-esteem. Men make mistakes and admit them. Men are determined to achieve. Men respect themselves and others. Men don't whine, though on occasion they might cry. Men do all they can to maintain independence. Men make wise choices. Men are motivated.

All of these traits of manhood can be consciously developed. Men start acquiring them as young men, and when they are faced with negative behaviors, they must draw the line. They must not become involved in activities which are self-destructive and which do not lead to manhood.

The pride which young Black men feel when others speak of them as "fine or outstanding young men" is a great feeling. Manhood is to strive for this recognition.

Chapter 6
Young Black Men and Fatherhood

All things are possible for those who believe.
Bible Passage
Lawrence J. Hanks
Dean, Afro-American Affairs
Indiana University

Many young Black men have experienced positive relationships with their own fathers. In these cases, they and their parents share a strong and loving bond which strengthens with progressive years.

Some, however, have not been so fortunate. Some hardly know their fathers. In many cases, there has been total neglect. No matter which kind of paternal relationship they_ve had, either type of father gives them reasons for becoming fathers themselves only when willing, capable, and anxious to become one in the best sense of the word. The relationship with their own father might have been so positive that they are eager to emulate that kind of relationship with their own children. Conversely, it might have been such a negative relationship that they are determined to create a father-role quite unlike the one experienced as a child.

Many young Black men seem to feel that they establish their "manhood" by becoming fathers. This is far from true. Fatherhood is a privilege that should require a strong commitment.

Animals reproduce when they are physically mature. People, on the other hand, should rely on other factors. They should consider parenting when they are capable of providing a wholesome, positive environment for their children.

Fathering a baby requires a strong desire on the part of the father to assure that the child will have every opportunity, which is the child's right, to develop properly and to become a responsible, productive adult. In order for this to happen, the father must be mature and in a position to provide for the physical and emotional needs of the child.

The behavior of "children" having children creates problems for both parents and society. Frequently it stifles a young woman's chance for personal advancement. It also creates problems for the father with the required contributions for rearing a child. Very rarely does anyone win in this situation.

There is nothing more beautiful than parenting. Fatherhood is a great phase of a man's life. It should be the result of joint planning and a strong desire to share in the rearing of a child in a loving environment. This is something every baby, and every father, deserves.

As I have talked with young men who have fathered children as teenagers, I have gotten the same general answers from all of them. "I love my child, but I wish that this had never happened," or "I would now have preferred that I would have been more mature and more capable of taking care of a child." There is a time for all events in life. Fatherhood should be the follow up of a loving relationship that, as a result of physical and emotional maturity, and financial security, culminates in expanding the family. It should be a choice made by potential parents who want and can properly support a child." True fatherhood requires a strong commitment.

A large percentage of inmates in prisons are victims of bad parenting. They grew up in settings without male role models. When "children are rearing children," there are innumerable problems.

If the father does attempt to assume responsibility, he must earn a living. His plans for further education then must be put on hold, however, his income potential is greatly reduced. Frequently during that time, although the young man verbalizes that he's going back to school, he frequently finds himself trapped in a rut — often within a few years, he's fathered a second and sometimes more children, each adding to expenses, and further limiting personal growth and advancement. When you look at the disadvantages of teenage fatherhood and attempt to list advantages, there is a wide discrepancy between the two columns. I could list not a single advantage.

Chapter 7
No Excuses

Although tremendous progress has been made, there is much left to do in order for African American males to realize the American dream. You must be prepared to take advantage of the opportunities that now exist. You must always do your best. No excuse is ever good enough for not doing your best at all times.

You must be prepared to push back the remaining frontiers in every aspect of American life.

You must construct a vision for your life. It is imperative that you always have something significant yet to do in the future, because a powerful vision of the future is what gives meaning to life.

Remember, when you construct that vision, you must act on it, because as one authority has said, "Vision without action is merely dreaming; action without vision just passes time; but vision with action can change the world." You can change the world!

Thomas E. Kerns, Ed.D.
Superintendent
Greenville County School District

One of the situations which I have seen and which bothers me greatly is that of young Black men using "race" as an excuse for not achieving. I am aware that in the not too distant past, inequalities in educational facilities, materials, and equipment contributed toward an unequal education between races. The United States Supreme Court banned segregated schools in 1954. Although there was no immediate compliance, more than forty years have passed since that time. The very effective Headstart Program has assisted greatly in closing the gap, and some gaps remain due to economics. Jobs for many Black men are still at the lower rung of the ladder. Income is relatively low. Encyclopedias and other resources are not on the shelves in many lower income homes. Although public libraries are a little less convenient to reach than bookshelves at home, they are there, and they do provide tools essential to academic achievement.

One comment I have heard from white teachers referring to Black students even through the high school level is: "He's so cute." Being "cute" is not a complimentary adjective as far as I'm concerned. Being "cute" or being "funny" are not terms which should cause a young man to feel proud. He's so "capable" or he's so "smart" would be more appropriate qualities to which you should aspire.

I know that most young Black men have the ability to achieve well with moderate effort. I know that with more effort their achievement level will be even greater. I have no doubt all of them can reach their goals if they really work toward them. Many people put in a lot of time and effort attempting to beat the system. With this same energy directed purposefully toward achievement, the accomplishments attained will be surprising.

There are reasons why persons sometimes feel that they aren't given a fair shake and are not treated fairly. I understand that. I know that in many cases it's true. We might think of our own ancestors, and the many abuses which were thrust upon them, and their survival skills. We can bring the period forward to the civil rights movement and see the doors of entry to various colleges barred for Blacks. We can see restaurants, hotels, and other areas of public accommodation which were exclusive of Blacks. We can look at housing patterns and areas of cities where Black people were relegated. People of yesterday used their intelligence and pressed on and demanded change.

The way to effect change, to assure fair treatment, is through education and preparation. Young Black men must arm themselves with an education so that they can demand the respect that they have earned.

There are so many opportunities to make excuses. We have all made them, and we have all heard them. I could probably put all the excuses which I have heard into about a dozen categories and number them. Thousands given would fall neatly into one of the dozen. Why make excuses when they are unnecessary.

I have heard the excuse from some Black young men that "I didn't get the job because I'm Black." I don't doubt that there are some prejudiced employers. I also don't doubt that sometimes the lack of qualification is the real issue.

I strongly encourage young Black men to set goals, look at requirements, and take personal inventories. What are my current qualifications to reach the goal? What is missing, or what do I need yet to be totally capable of reaching the goal? Then, start filling the voids. Reach a goal, then set new ones.

All of us are responsible for our own behavior. We cannot conduct ourselves in improper ways and blame others for the misconduct. We must take credit or blame for all the things we do. Final decisions are ours individually and ours alone.

You will find that the rewards of accomplishment and of goal reaching are so self-satisfying that they are far superior to excuse making. There is no substitute for self-esteem. There is no simpler way to acquire or embellish it than through personal achievement.

What will you do when you grow up? This is a question that is asked all of us at various stages in life. Young boys might reply, "Fireman," "Policeman," "Pilot," or some other exciting career. As time goes by and adolescence is reached, the answers may change to, "Doctor," "Lawyer," "Business owner," and other high-salary professions. Then high school years come and reality sets in. Unless you have been seriously considering your future and building a solid foundation, you have some repair work to do. It's impossible to put a second story on a basement. You have to fill in the void and stabilize the structure.

If a young Black man allowed himself to become a junior in high school with weak math or English skills, continuing to attempt to climb without simultaneously strengthening weak skills will be counter-productive. As he begins to correct deficiencies, he will bridge the gap and be able to climb considerably higher without limitations.

When asked what career choice he plans to follow, he will be able to respond based upon desire without having to say, "I would have been a doctor, but I did poorly in math and science in high school."

Young men can follow their dream based upon their determination to make things happen.

Somehow many young Black men seem to have a bag of excuses. Sometimes even the slave heritage of yesteryear is used as the scapegoat of young Black men in the 20th century. Lack of academic performance, lack of good study habits, lack of acceptable reading skills are all explained with the excuse that someone else did not "give me the opportunity."

One main point which I hope young Black men understand is that they individually are responsible for themselves. Rather than "they did this to me," it should be "I accepted what was done." You are the captain of your ship. Your destiny is determined by you.

In every community there are positive Black men who reach out to assist young Black men. Nevertheless, many prefer to follow the negative leaders in the community. Many positive role models are professionals such as teachers, attorneys, physicians, engineers, and insurance reps. Others are athletes who want to give back to their communities.

As young Black men, you have a debt. You owe the Black men and women who have fought and died to secure freedom and opportunity for Black people in this country. You owe the freedom riders, the men and women who participated in sit-ins so that you might enter restaurants and expect service, you owe those who have fought for open housing so that you may live in any neighborhood you can afford, you owe many for the job opportunities as a result of their fight for employment opportunities.

Your payment of these debts is not in money. Your payment is made through your own conduct. As you personally make your payments through achievement, through positive attitudes and through serving as role models for other Black youth. You are paying a debt in a manner which would inspire those who have gone before you to have great pride.

We have long been victims of racism. The heritage we have and the strong will and determination of our ancestors give us strength and power.

We have always had strong leaders who have managed to continue our fight for justice through the years. Each generation has profited from the untiring efforts of previous generations. Through hard work, education and strong leadership, many closed doors have been opened.

I have found that the secret to achievement is through education. I have also learned that when persons achieve, and become more independent, the forces of racism are appreciably reduced. Racist attitudes are intolerable. When as young people you react to racist attitudes with loud raucous behavior, you are responding as the racist would desire. It is better to show your intelligence and confront the irrational nature of racism.

Chapter 8
Ingredients for Success

There are no long term short cuts to success. You must work hard and earn everything you get in life.

Allan Browder, President
Browder Restaurants, Inc.
Kansas City, Missouri

It's so easy to loaf, to sit back and take it easy. It's somewhat harder to focus on accomplishment, but the rewards are great. We all have watched football games and have seen some unusual plays made by young men who refused to be tackled. We have seen underdog boxers win their bouts. The difference has been a determination to accomplish.

This same kind of determination can be applied to academic achievement, to your social conduct, in fact to every facet of your life. The football player who continues to run, who eludes the tacklers, who determines to reach the goal and scores, is just an example of a motivated and determined person.

Each of you has potential for achievement. The reasons why some achieve and others don't are due to motivation and determination.

SOME DO'S AND DON'T'S FOR YOUNG BLACK MEN
1. Hold your head high. You have many reasons to show pride.
2. Give a firm handshake to others and show that you feel good about yourself.
3. Respect yourself and you will demand respect from others.
4. Being macho does not mean disrespect to girls and women.
5. Personal appearance is a means of presenting yourself. Your appearance says to others, "This is me." Present yourself as you want to be accepted.

6. The most important personal attribute which you must acquire is self-esteem. You honestly feel good about yourself only when you deserve to.
7. You have many positive Black role models. Select some of them.
8. Don't follow leaders who have negative goals.
9. Be cautious as you select your friends. There's an old saying: "Show me your company and I'll tell you who you are."
10. Remember how hard your ancestors fought for your civil rights. Work equally hard to achieve and make life better for those who will follow you.
11. You must take steps to achieve positive goals. When you jump too quickly and too high you miss some important points.
12. You owe it to others to become a positive role model.
13. Realize the importance of reading. Use your mind in a positive way.
14. Be a leader not a follower.
15. If you do follow, follow only good leaders.
16. Don't use excuses.
17. Always remember that no peer can make you do anything.
18. Always have short-term goals and each day take steps toward achieving them.
19. Never accept mediocrity.
20. Keep away from gang or mob action.
21. Maintain an "I can do it" attitude.
22. Don't give up easily. Work diligently to achieve.
23. Remember that the best weapon which you have is your brain.
24. Respect yourself and you will demand respect from others.
25. Respect others and you will personally feel a greater sense of worth.
26. Be positive with your personal attitude. Being pleasant pays dividends.
27. Establish high expectations.
28. Walk with a purpose.
29. Read worthwhile books.

Change doesn't come about easily. Consistent effort is necessary to effect change. And there *first* must be the realization that you need to change. Persons ought to take a personal inventory. Ask yourself, "What do I want out of life? What are the really good qualities which I possess?" Write down the list. You'll be surprised at the number of positive qualities.

Think about qualities which keep you from reaching your goals. Make a list of them. Writing these positive and negative qualities will give you a benchmark from which to work.

It isn't expected that all negative changes will be corrected overnight. If a person practices consistently to make individual changes, the feedback he will receive from those who know him will be so rewarding that determination to further improve himself will be increased.

There's an old saying, "Fly with the crows. Get shot with the crows." We inescapably are affected by the close associations we have with others. If we surround ourselves with people who have goals, who waste little time, who involve themselves in worthwhile activities, our chances of developing these traits will be great.

On the other hand, if we associate with others who have no positive goals, and frequently are in trouble at home, school or community, our likelihood for developing a negative behavior pattern will also be strong. The quicker a person decides his own fate, the quicker he determines for himself that he really wants to be somebody, the greater chance he will have of getting there.

We have all heard comments, "Boy, he's really lucky." If we knew the facts, we would realize that most accomplishment is not through luck, but rather through perseverance, determination, goal setting and hard work. It's never too late to take that road, but we can't have it both ways. Either we decide a positive goal is important and work toward it with diligence, or we show inconsistency and work half-heartedly toward achieving a goal.

Some young Black men probably already have some positive role models. What are the reasons that one person selects a particular person as a model? Is it someone who has accomplished something through diligence, or is it someone who drives a big car, has flashy gold chains, is unemployed and involved in illegal activities?

Success is a nebulous term. What are the measures of success? If I were to ask that question randomly, I would get a wide variety of responses. Some would equate success with monetary attainments. Some would consider success in light of personal satisfaction. All persons should strive to reach successful plateaus. They should set attainable goals, accomplish them, and then reach for higher ones. They have a personal obligation to "be the best that they can be." We are all aware of the stereotypical Black male as carefree, uninhibited, non-motivated, lazy, undisciplined. Each time one follows that path, he perpetuates the myth.

I have talked with many Black men who are motivated and are successful in their occupations. Many of them have come from settings which would suggest that the attainment of high goals would be unlikely. Many of them have come from single parent, low income homes. Many have grown up in sub-standard housing. Yet, frequently the single parent home is filled with love, demands responsibility, and motivates the young man to "reach." In other words, those who use their status as a reason for not achieving are too frequently merely making excuses. It might, of course, require extra effort, but it can be done.

There are many factors which contribute to our successes and failures. It is my strong belief that we are individually in control of our own destiny. Young Black men owe it to themselves to assure that their lives will be positive and personally fulfilled ones.

I had the privilege of spending three years on a committee for the National Merit Corporation. Our role was to determine very objectively the National Achievement Scholarship Semi-Finalists. The National Achievement Program is a special program which awards merit scholarships to minority students. As I reviewed the personal background of many students being considered for the prestigious awards, I was amazed at the high grades achieved in very demanding courses by most of the students. All had qualified for competition through competitive testing. There were, of course, many who grew up in professional home settings, who had many privileges. There were many others, however, who in spite of obvious obstacles, had qualified as Achievement Scholars.

Just as that group became Achievement Scholars and eligible for scholarships, so can many other young Black men. Dr. Mary McLeod Bethune, founder and former president of Bethune-Cookman College, was a sought-after speaker nationwide. I was fortunate to have heard her speak during my first year in college. I have never forgotten her speech titled, "Young Folks, Do Something, Be Somebody." I challenge you with that same thought.

Young men need to know early where they are going and the necessary things which they must accomplish, and they must keep a direct route to reach their goals. Some, of course, take many unnecessary detours, but eventually reach the desired goal. Many young men, however, don't seem to have goals in mind. They go, so to speak, with the flow. Since the men who have had major problems have also had few goals, it would seem that the majority of them would select the best route.

"But you don't know what it's like." That statement is given frequently by young Black men to older Black men who attempt to help them to improve their behavior. Granted, we don't know the "drug scene" and the "Black on Black crime scene" or the high rate of crime generally, but we have been exposed to the many prejudices and attitudes which have been a bitter part of our heritage. Over against this kind of abusive treatment, Black men have stood up, and with great pride have fought the civil rights battle for equal employment opportunities, for open housing, for integrated education and for open public accommodations. We have watched and been a part of the many changes which have occurred during the past several decades, and we are proud of many who have taken and are taking advantages of the opportunities which have resulted from these efforts.

On the other hand, we are deeply distressed by many of the negative things which we are more recently observing. Only you have it in your power to reverse the pattern. Only you have the capability to reject the negative destructive behavior which has become so common among many of our youth.

Young Black men have it within their power to be the Martin Luther King of their community. They have reasons to become leaders. We must realize that the current roles of many young Black men are not acceptable. A movement for change is necessary.

We have strategists with expert abilities to design a procedure. We are aware that we must displace criminal activity with positive behavior. I have seen young Black men in prison who are achieving academically, completing high school, college and even some graduate and professional specialization. These men are capable. Why prison schools? Why correspondence courses with institutions while inmates? Why not eliminate need for incarceration and continue with your education in regular educational settings?

Instead of forming gangs for criminal activity, why not be a leader with a determination to achieve in school? Young Black men should share their talents with other young Black men. Many outstanding artists are Black men; many have great mechanical abilities. There are many, of course, who have great academic potential. If they were to really think about themselves and encourage friends to follow a path of achievement, they would be surprised to see what a difference they might make. Martin Luther King as a young man did not say, "I'm going to be the major force in a Civil Rights Movement," Booker T. Washington did not say, "In 1881, I'm going to organize a college and call it Tuskegee Institute." Neither Benjamin Davis nor Colin Powell said early in their lives they were going to become U.S. Generals. All of these men did, as young men, realize the importance of education and discipline, no matter what area of specialty to which they later aspired.

I cannot over-emphasize the necessity for young Black men to not only continue with their education, but to take their classes seriously, and perform in a commendable manner. As you read the advice from a variety of Black men preceding each chapter, in all cases education was important to the writer.

Chapter 9
Ingredients for Failure

1. Quit school early in life.
2. If you don't quit school totally, skip frequently.
3. Hang around with a group who cares little about themselves or their achievements.
4. Experiment with drugs or alcohol.
5. Get involved with activities which get you in trouble with legal authorities.
6. Show disrespect to your parents and other adults.
7. Spend more of your time in the streets or parks than in productive activities.
8. Spend an inordinate amount of time watching television.
9. Don't read newspapers or worthwhile books.
10. Don't set positive, achievable goals.

I have heard persons say, as they have spoken highly of particular Black men who have become real leaders, "I can't believe that's the same young man I knew earlier. He sure made a terrific turnaround." Of course we all make mistakes, some more major than others. It's never too late to make the changes needed to become successful. If you've allowed yourself to get involved in serious trouble, you should allow yourself the opportunity to straighten up and improve your conduct. A man is not indicted for life because of one major mistake, but a man indicts himself when he wallows in the mistake.

There are, however, limits to the numbers of chances we get. If a young Black man makes blunder after blunder and seems not to care about himself or others, then most likely he will find himself in serious trouble.

It's much easier to correct a problem if it hasn't gone too far. It's easier to find a way back before a lot of strange turns and detours. You will find that many people want to see you become successful and to help you to find your way. You will also find that many others who are taking the wrong route are thrilled to have you join them.

Remember the saying, "Show me your company, and I'll tell you who you are."

Chapter 10

Young Black Men and Conformity

A winner never quits. Always have goals and continue to strive to achieve them. If you reach for the moon, you will still be among the stars if you fall short. Those who succeed in life are the ones who work hard to be the best that they can be. Even if you are a turtle you can pass the hare in the race of life. Hold your head high and keep on keeping on.

Judge Charles A. Shaw

Peer pressure is a dominating influence on many people through out their lives. All people conform to social requirements of various types. We dress much the same, we listen to similar kinds of music, we socialize in certain places such as shopping malls for young people. We learn early in life that there are times and places for our various activities and appearances. If we use slang when we talk with our friends, during job interviews we dispense with that kind language.

There are many faddish modes of dress — during the last decade wearing baseball caps came into popularity. There is, of course, nothing wrong with wearing headgear as an outside garment, but somehow someone decided that headgear would also be worn inside buildings. You can see caps in homes, in school, perhaps even inside places of worship. This kind of behavior is an example of someone starting and others following a practice which shows little respect for tradition or others_ expectations of appropriate behavior.

Life is a series of short journeys. We all take different routes, we travel in different kinds of vehicles, but we all should strive for reaching worthwhile destinations. If a person is planning a trip, he makes a schedule. The same thing should be true with his life's journey. He must have a plan and he must follow the scheduled routes. Sometimes we take detours. Sometimes we think we can bypass some necessary route. However, by taking detours, we lose several years of our lives to counter-productive activities and behaviors. Reconsider your situation if you have the thought, "I'm only going to skip one day," "I'm only going to call in this one time and not go to work," "I'll tell them I'm sick," "I'm only going to stay out all night just once," "I'm only going to run around with this crowd for tonight," "Stealing from my mom's purse is easy, I'll just do it one time, or "'Doing drugs only one time can't hurt me."

We take detours and, if we continue practicing negative behavior, we end up with our lives being truly scarred. Young Black men must take advantage of every opportunity to stay on the right road for reaching their goals. They have the ability to make life truly worthwhile. When they are older men and have the opportunity to review their own life's journey, they will have a earned a feeling of pride.

I realize that for young Black men, projecting that far ahead might be asking too much, yet their chances for accomplishment will be greatly enhanced if they envision their future. They must ask themselves individually, what would I like to be doing in two years? Five years? What accomplishments would I want to have achieved at the end of ten years? Twenty years? What do I need to do to reach these levels of attainment?

Chapter 11
The Pseudo Leader

Young Black men today are faced with many unique challenges. My message is to set goals early and always very high. Find out everything possible about each step in achieving goals, plan them out, even write them detailing each step and follow them. I have found that success comes not by chance but by careful and deliberate planning.

Alphonso Robinson
Pharmacist
Tuskegee, Alabama

All of us have met the loud-talking, know-it-all person who seems to have the skill of attracting followers. He frequently has the ability to perform well in school but defies authority and does not apply himself with study. Instead, he undermines the positive elements around him. Why others follow him is not easy to understand.

There are, on the other hand, young men who are determined to achieve.

As young Black men consider the kinds of leaders they will follow, they should think about their friends, and objectively think of themselves and the qualities which they most admire in each. Are the majority of their friends real leaders or pseudo ones? Many of the young men in prison really are leaders. As I have met with them, I have been able to identify leadership qualities which have been misdirected. I have also seen the evidence of misdirected leadership abilities among young men in high school and college.

A true leader shows consistency with his practice of leadership. A true leader is aware of the power which he has and is cautious that that power is not misused.

Chapter 12
Positive Role Models

1. Be confident in one's ability to succeed.
2. Draw all you can from models at home, church, school for values.
3. Education, education, education.
4. Assume racism and then go on to the next part of your life.
5. Give back, give back and give back to those behind you.

- K.C. Morrison, Vice Chancellor
University of Missouri

Who is truly a "hero" or "role model"? How important is it to have these figures in your life?

A hero conducts himself in a manner worthy of respect and admiration. A hero conducts himself in a way which others emulate.

As we grow, it's important to have role models for our motivation. We change heroes as our interests change. Growing up as very young men, for example, we might look up to specific athletes. As we gain more maturity and widen our focus, our heroes may be those whose achievements and accomplishments are more in line with our specific interests. As we develop interests in areas such as music, science, or politics, our heroes might well be accomplished persons in our specific areas of interest. Sometimes the hero might emerge because of qualities we admire and has little to do with occupations or special interests.

We all need positive role models. Role modeling serves several purposes. Young men and women who are developing their own personal values and who have personal yardsticks will be assisted by having these standards. Role models themselves who are in position to gain the respect of young people are obligated to conduct themselves in a manner which deserves respect. It's an effective deterrent to misconduct.

The "hero" for young people should look upon that designation as a real honor. There are few greater honors that persons might receive than to have others who sincerely look up to them as role models.

What generally are the traits of the men that you look up to? Some positive traits are strong character, a commitment to achieve, a desire to help others as they climb, strong family involvement, and high levels of motivation.

These kinds of positive traits rarely begin at mid-life. Young men need to make decisions early about themselves and work daily towards attaining the goals of the decisions. It's never too early to begin. If a person begins now to practice self-discipline, to think for himself instead of following the crowd, to keep positive goals, he will very likely attain the goals. These positive traits will be his permanent personal logo.

As young Black men are growing and developing, and as they wisely select their own role models, I fervently hope that they will look beyond money and flashy cars as symbols of success. I hope that they will have the capacity to see beyond the material showcase. If, on the other hand, they equate success with the attainment of positive goals, their understanding of the term "success" is a realistic one.

When a person understands real success, he could list those men who fall in the category of "successful" and then select his role models. He can take the list down to possibly five or six, look at them very carefully and then ask, "Which three are really *my* role models?"

A model is just that. A person doesn't have to become a clone, but can admire the attributes of the other person. He should want to start early in developing some of the same qualities. The hero didn't become the kind of person he is overnight. Instead, he slowly acquired these qualities.

One of my personal memories which helped me to realize the effectiveness of modeling is of an event that occurred five years ago. My wife and I were parking in front of the post office when a man driving by yelled out my name, parked his truck on the other side of the street, ran across, shook my hand and said, "Mr. Battle, I want to thank you. If it hadn't been for you I wouldn't have made it in life."

I felt very gratified, of course, but after a few minutes of talk, he thanked me again, went to his truck, pulled off and drove away. I mailed my letter and came back to the car. My wife asked, "Who was that and what did you do?" I could not recall the answer to either. This reinforced my knowledge that modeling cannot be a superficial act, yet may be done almost impersonally by setting an example in your community.

If you are to be a positive role model or to select a role model, you must be cautious and select a person who understands who and what he represents.

As young Black men think about their role models, they should also consider for whom they might be serving as models. They have an obligation to conduct themselves in such a manner that as their younger brothers look up to them, that they are looking up to a positive role model. The language that they use, the respect which they show their mothers and other women, the self-respect that they exhibit — all of these are being viewed daily by their younger brothers. There is no greater feeling than when a younger brother wants to be like you for positive reasons.

Chapter 13
Young Black Male School Dropouts

Stay in school, and take care of yourself spiritually and physically.

Johnny Ford, Mayor
Tuskegee, Alabama

What are young people thinking when they consider dropping out from school? What advantages do young Black men see in such an act? We all know that opportunities for advancement usually come to those who have shown perseverance in their education. We find increased opportunities in life in direct proportion to academic achievement. Even so, in almost every community throughout the country, we find young Black men merely "hanging out." If these young men directed their energy towards the attainment of positive goals, their accomplishments would be mind-boggling.

There were times in the past when a Black high school graduate and a school dropout had much the same employment opportunities — building maintenance, cooking, and other service occupations. That time has passed. Young Black men with specific skills are sought out by potential employers. As a result of civil rights marches and demonstrations, these opportunities have become yours. To have the opportunity to reach worthwhile goals, and to turn your backs on these opportunities, are negative responses to the sacrifices of your ancestors.

As a student makes choices, he should do so with a plan. The correct way to make a decision is to consider all options. One does not just think about them. That way it's easy to overlook some important aspects of an issue. The best approach to a decision is to list options on paper. Put the title of the decision under consideration, then list the pros and cons of that decision, that is, the reasons you should and the reasons you shouldn't. Then, objectively review the two lists. A decision made in this manner is much more meaningful than one hastily made. Before finalizing the decisions, talk to someone you respect and note their responses.[3]

EXAMPLE
Should I drop out of school?

Reasons why:
- I can get a job and make some money
- I will limit my further training possibilities
- I will not be qualified for the armed services
- I'm tired of school and my friends have quit

Reasons why not:
- If I don't quit but study and do well, I will get a much better job and make more money
- I might decide to go on to a vocational school or college or even the armed services
- How long will I have these same friends?
- I'll be a disappointment to my family

Chapter 14
Pride

Be responsible and accept responsibility. Education is critical to your development and future success. Drugs and alcohol destroy your potential and assure that you will always be a second-rate citizen.

Richard Holmes, M.D.
Vice President for Development
Dupont-Merck Pharmaceutical Company

When I was a student at Tuskegee University during the 1940s, I was fortunate to meet many Tuskegee airmen who were in training as part of the 99th Pursuit Squadron. Among the men I met was General Benjamin O. Davis, Jr., a man who reached many heights during his career. Simply knowing the man was an honor. It is with great pride that I include him as one of my personal heroes. If I had never heard General Davis utter a word, or if I had not known of his flying and teaching skills, I still would have admired him for his personal demeanor. In his highly decorated uniform standing with shoulders erect, whose total appearance said to young teenagers, "Look at me. I'm Black and I'm proud." – his pride was contagious. It caused many young Tuskegee students to hold their shoulders back and to show pride in themselves. I know I was among them.

In growing up, we all go through various phases. No one makes it without some problems. Those who survive problems without scars are those who work hard at doing so. Adolescence is a tough time for both the adolescent and for the parents or guardians. During adolescence, patience and understanding are needed. It is during that period that young people make decisions, many of which turn out to have been wrong. These are the periods when heroes and mentors are important. Improper choices and negative heroes can prove to be very detrimental.

When people select persons they admire, they should examine them closely and be sure that their qualities are worthy of admiration. It's important to have models, yet it's equally important that these models have a proven track record.

There are some personal qualities common to all Black men respected in their local communities throughout the nation. These qualities include self-esteem, interest in others, earned trust. They are men of character, visionaries — they are not phonies.

There are, likewise, some personal qualities which are common to all Black men who are not respected. They lack self-esteem; they are self-centered; they are not trustworthy; they lack character; they see no further than the tips of their noses — they are phony.

It would seem that any young man in looking at the two descriptions would automatically opt for the first. Yet men who fit the second description attract a large following of young Black men. One of the major reasons is that they are generally more visible. They are frequently unemployed and are hanging around often in the same areas where teens congregate.

You are a young Black man. You could be a young white man, an Asian man, or a young native-American man, but you are none of these. You are a young Black man. You are very special. You have great reason to be a proud young Black man.

As we read daily papers and view scenes on television of Black youth in elementary and junior high school involved in violent criminal activity, we shudder. Who's responsible? There is no one answer. All of society can feel responsible for human tragedy.

Young Black men have a specific responsibility, however. They serve as role models to the Black children in their communities, many at an age when playing with toys would be appropriate behavior. Instead they are using guns, stealing cars, or involved in the drug scene.

We are all different. Some appear to have had a much easier road to travel than others. I know that obstacles can make a difference with performance. I know also that the more obstacles and problems a young man has, the more challenging it is for him to continue with positive progress.

For some, as the poet Langston Hughes says, "Life for me ain't been no crystal stair." In spite of a bumpy road, many young Black men achieve. The difference is attitude, determination, persistence, drive, and refusal to accept defeat. It takes a strong person to make it in spite the adversity.

Chapter 15
Goal Setting

Life in prison is hard. "I wish I had the chance to back up and undo the act that caused me to be here;" and "I wish that I had listened to those who were my real friends, my mom, my teacher, my coach and others who tried to get me to study and to stay in school with a positive focus." These were the typical comments I heard when I talked with young men in prison.

Although the problems which young Black men face in today's society seem insurmountable, it seems the least desirable option to commit a crime which might lead to incarceration.

It would also seem that with the accomplishments attained by young Black men who are determined to achieve and who go the college route, this would inspire young Black men to emulate that route to success.

There are thousands of highly motivated young Black men in our country who make positive strides. There are thousands more who involve themselves in shady activities and ultimately end up in prison. You have a responsibility to yourselves to join ranks with the positive achievers.

The three essentials of success are **motivation, preparation** and **contact**. One must have a drive to make something of his life — well-defined goals and motivations to reach those goals. Next, he must diligently prepare himself by going to school, learning, studying regularly, and becoming as knowledgeable as possible. In the process of doing this he must impress himself upon those individuals who will be able to say a good word for and about him.

He must always remember that footprints on the sand of time are never made while sitting down.

Jack Rackley
Professor of Education (Ret.)
Florida A & M University
Tallahassee, Florida

All of you have heard the statement, "You can make it if you try." Some of you probably think of this as being corny. Let me assure you that effort does make a difference. We may be discouraged by our peers saying, "You won't be able to do that." If little confidence in our abilities is shown by others, our efforts to achieve may be diluted. When we use doubt as a challenge, we find the effort to succeed pays off. When we show little confidence in ourselves, even greater problems emerge. Low confidence promotes low self-esteem. Persons with low self-esteem do not reach their potential.

Think about your friends. You may have thought "I wish I were as smart as a particular friend." Though you, too, are basically smart, you may not be using those smarts to your advantage.

Many young Black men have lifted weights and felt that they have done so to their capacity, or have done push-ups and felt that they'd reached their limit. Then they say to themselves, "I'll go ten more, then ten more." They finally reach their capacity, but not before they have done considerably more than originally intended.

The same kind of determination can and should be a part of their academic training. This is a part of goal setting and planning. It's easy to give in, find yourself not achieving, continue in that direction, and fall through the cracks. It's important not to let that happen. It's important to keep personal goals high, work consistently toward them and make something positive of your life.

Why do some young Black men with adverse circumstances succeed in life whereas others who appear to have everything going for them follow a negative route? It's up to each person to set their own standards and reach up and make a difference with themselves. There's a real problem when persons allow "things" to interfere with their achievements. When persons let such obstacles as drugs, alcohol, illegal behavior, lack of interest, or peers dictate to them and cause them to not make positive growth and development, they are really doing great harm to themselves and to their future families.

There is no prescription for the qualities all young men must develop in order to reach positive goals. Various amounts at different times would be needed for individuals. There are some basics, however, that if followed, would contribute greatly toward reaching successful points in life. Some of them include:

1. A positive attitude
2. Determination to succeed
3. Setting and working toward positive goals
4. Consistency with efforts
5. No backsliding
6. Associating with persons who have positive goals
7. Avoiding problem situations

Think about these qualities. What is meant by a positive attitude? One needn't grin from ear to ear to be positive. One should look at the world in such a manner as to say, "I can do it," and really mean it. Determination suggests an attitude of letting nothing stop you from reaching your goals. Positive goals and working toward them are important to you if you're going to be successful.

It is important that each person sets reachable or attainable goals. Working consistently toward goals should be practiced. There can be no backsliding if you're going to make progress. A person can't take three steps forward and six steps backward and expect to accomplish his goals. One way to assure reaching goals is to maintain an association with others who also have worked and continue to work toward higher aspirations. Such association is stimulating. And by all means, stay away from trouble. Don't put yourself in situations that can create problems for yourself or others.

Young Black men must not be victims. A young Black man is not always responsible for the events happening to him. He is, however, responsible for his own reactions to these things. If our forefathers had chosen other responses to past obstacles, think of possible outcomes. If Black men had not had the foresight and courage to establish institutions of higher learning, imagine what we might be doing even today. If Black men had not held their heads high and defied civic segregation, we would still have greater problems. Look at the opportunities which are rightfully ours. If we do not take advantage of positive opportunities, we are failing ourselves and our forefathers.

What qualities must be developed if success is expected? One must be motivated to become successful, and have attainable goals. It is important that goals be both short and long term. As a person thinks about his future, he could easily become discouraged with a long term goal if he did not have a series of intermittent short term reachable goals. It's important if he plans to become a certified auto mechanic requiring post-high school training to set a goal completing an auto mechanics program while still in high school.

Why do some make it and others not? What terms describe both types? Which is more like you? Is it the way you want to be? How can you change it? Sometimes, we need to look at ourselves honestly and resist throwing our arms up in futility. Sometimes, if a person took just one more positive step, it could make all the difference in his life. If people stood up for their beliefs, eliminating negative peer pressure, their futures could be changed appreciably.

There are extremely negative courses which many follow and extremely positive courses followed by others, and there are many varied in-between routes. I have found that the more positive routes lead to more positive goals.

Chapter 16
Self Worth

Perseverance Pursue your dreams. Don't give up. Focus try again, try again.

Kit Carson Roque
Municipal Court Judge
Kansas City, Missouri

Over a period of many years, as I have observed young Black men, I have often been able to determine their feelings about themselves even without conversation. Their posture as they sit or stand, the way they hold their heads up with pride or look downward with little esteem, and the way they look into the eyes of others with whom they communicate, each of these nonverbal indicators reveals secrets about people. Of course, the same things can be said of all people in general, but I have especially noticed young Black men as they show these signs.

Self worth is crucial to all of us. How does each person value himself? Are they aware that if they think of themselves as worthless and act worthless, they will be treated as such. In their conduct, if they show that they value themselves, conduct themselves in a manner that suggests that they feel they are persons of worth, they will find that others will also see them in that light and their respect for them will be proportionately higher.

Many young Black men have grown up in homes without fathers. They need support from male relatives, family friends, schools, churches and community organizations like Big Brothers. Many growing up in this type of environment gain independence early and develop into very competent and successful adults. Others use their background as an excuse for not conducting themselves positively. This is really not grounds for failure. Many have proven otherwise.

All men have opportunities. Some wallow in self-pity and don't take advantage of opportunities. Others seem to gain greater determination and refuse to accept any obstacles.

Each person must practice positive behavior and not give in to negative conduct.

What are young Black men's chances for a successful future? It might seem simple to answer that it all depends on them, but that is the answer I offer. I know from experience as well as from observation that Black men can climb to great heights. I know also that it is a very demanding climb summoning all kinds of personal resources.

During my lifetime, I have met thousands of Black men who have achieved varied measures of success. There are some special traits that they all possess: they refused to give up; they were determined; they were purposeful; and they took no short-cuts. In other words, they took each step at a time.

I have watched failure resulting from efforts to take the easy way out. There are those who look at a goal, see their starting point, then jump too quickly and stumble. Others at that same starting point climb each step, learn each process, and enter into the realm of success. This is an important point to remember. Don't skip necessary steps.

How one budgets his time throughout the school year and during the summer is important. Each person must realize the importance of achievement. He must also realize the importance of daily study. If you're out of high school, do you realize the importance of continued development through reading, seminars, short courses, and other learning activities? These activities must be prioritized. Basketball, football, track, music and other extracurricular activities all contribute toward character and development. They should, if desired, be included. They should not displace the most important event of your growth and development: academic achievement.

All normal Black youth have the ability to reach great heights. Some require a little more study time than others to reach the same levels, but with perseverance it can be done.

Chapter 17
Purpose

The destiny of our society is rooted in God's word the Bible. Not excluding any other success, cultures, the improvement of our lot as Black men will be determined by (1) our willingness to embrace and practice the spiritual and moral principles found within the Bible. (2) valuing the family structure as a means to not only perpetuate our genealogies, but to also contribute to building strong communities, states, countries and nations and (3) valuing education as a means to attaining resources for a good quality of life. Finally, for anything we have gained as an advantage, give some back to those who are disadvantaged.

Charles Brown, Executive Director
State and Federal Programs
St. Louis Public Schools

All of us have a purpose in life. Some of us identify early for ourselves what that purpose is and plot appropriate strategies to achieve the purpose. Others, on the other hand, do not map out a plan. If we examine carefully, we find that those who reach positive goals have been careful in their planning. They have identified their goals, they have selected the best routes to reach them, and they have made great efforts to attain them. We must therefore follow these strategies if we are going to be successful in our endeavors.

Look around your community and identify the Black men who are successful. Stop by their offices or businesses and tell them that you would like to introduce yourself to them, and you would appreciate it if they would share with you their reasons for achievement and their most important elements contributing toward their success.

As you listen to the variety of reasons, think how frequently you listen to "the importance of education." If this is generally looked upon by most achievers, it would seem that as a young Black man you would not allow anything to interfere with your acquiring a good education.

It is my personal philosophy that each generation owes the previous one to improve upon their achievements. I feel very proud when I hear a young Black man say, "I'm a first generation college student." Because college has not been the avenue followed by relatives need not be a reason for you to feel that you share the same fate. As Mary McLeod Bethune suggested, you should make a decision to, "Do something. Be somebody."

There is no such word, as far as I'm concerned, as "can't." If you practice your activities with that same philosophy, you'll be able to reach many goals.

Three of the areas which must be considered by young Black men as they develop are personal, social and academic. Each of them is very important and should be given much emphasis.

Personal growth and habits contribute greatly toward the kind of person that each of you will become. If you participate in positive activities, your chances of personal success will be greatly enhanced. In addition, if in your social behavior you keep your interaction with others on a positive level, you likewise keep on a positive level. This will contribute greatly toward good results.

As you increase your chances for success, both personally and socially, and compound this with academic determination, your likelihood of achieving well is practically guaranteed. People usually achieve as a result of careful planning. Sometimes we look at persons who achieve, who seem not to have definite goals. Let me assure you they do. They sometimes are studying while others are sleeping.

As earlier stated, many young Black teenagers are on a positive path. Many have set goals early and have continued to realize the necessity for reaching toward them. Many are college bound, are taking the necessary courses for college entrance and potential college success. They are meeting with their high school counselors and are keeping up with all requirements, including financial aid possibilities, so that when the time arrives they will be ready.

Other young Black teenagers are shirking their responsibilities. They are enrolled in school and are taking the easiest of courses to get by but eventually receive a diploma comparable to an attendance certificate. It's easy to merely slide through. It's more important to your future that you follow a planned curriculum that is challenging and that will prepare you for successful college acceptance.

Your opportunities are great. The doors and avenues to many routes are wide open to you. In order to successfully achieve, you must have a solid foundation. You don't acquire that foundation through osmosis. You must really put out the effort and consistently study so that you will be prepared for any opportunity that presents itself. The roads to success are not always paved. Sometimes they are rocky and sometimes pitted, but with effort and determination you can successfully travel them.

There is no person who at some time has not suffered from discouragement. When a goal is set, and effort is put forth to reach it, and it's still not reached, that can be discouraging. Men who give up because of discouragement and do not attempt a second or a third endeavor will become disillusioned. They might stop attempting to achieve. It would be a big mistake to give up merely because of lack of accomplishing a goal.

There is no person who has not, at some time in his life, felt really good about accomplishing something worthwhile. It's a great feeling. When we look at the times of accomplishment and the times of discouragement, we of course prefer the goal-reaching. We know that the goals were reached because of consistent effort and purposefulness.

You should get in the habit of reviewing your individual purposes. This will give you the opportunity to see if you are truly on the right road. Sometimes altering the purpose will be desirable.

Chapter 18
Character Traits

Education is the key. Expand horizons beyond what is expected. Do not conform to stereotypes. Do not accept being average, strive for excellence. Do not be afraid to take a chance or accept a challenge if the reward is beneficial. Do not turn your back on your fellow Black males, everyone can use a helping hand if you have one to give. Please note: helping hand, not a handout.

Robert L. Davis
Bank President and CEO

Character traits are not inherited, they are adopted. When we hear people speak of others with such comments as, "He certainly has outstanding character," or "His character is without blemish," we feel really good. What is meant by an unblemished character? Persons of good character are persons who are not "Jeckyl and Hyde"s or "house angels and street devils." Instead, they are persons who have developed positive personal traits, they don't really have to give much thought to conduct. Acceptable behavior is a natural for them.

Since character is developed, character can be changed. There is no depth to which a person falls from which he cannot climb back up. Whatever your current situation, with strong character and determination you can made definite alterations. It's so easy to get down on yourself. One of the easiest things a person might do is to give up on himself. A person of character does not allow himself to stay down or to give up.

All of us have relatives or friends who have adopted character traits we admire. As we observe those who have desirable character traits, we should develop those traits for ourselves.

A young Black man who exhibits top character traits finds that those traits will assist him greatly in climbing the steps to success.

A man of high character thinks for himself and makes wise decisions. He walks with pride and seems to know where he's going. He thinks before he speaks. He considers consequences before he acts. He's considerate of others. He does not climb up while pushing others down, but tries to pull others along. Persons of good character are strong and do not give in to the whims of others. They follow their own convictions.

Chapter 19
Attitude

Always remember — America is still the land of opportunity.

Wilbur Robinson
Teacher
Tuskegee, Alabama

We all have dreams. We have the ability to make our dreams come true. The difference between those who achieve dreams and those who merely dream is attitude. If we are serious about accomplishing and achieving goals, we have to seriously plan strategies for reaching them. All of us have heard persons verbalize plans "I'm going to ... " but who always have an excuse for not accomplishing. It's so easy to be the procrastinator. Usually those kinds of people never seem to really hit the nail solidly on the head.

Young Black men should not fall into the trap of procrastinating. They must assure that they don't allow themselves the displeasure of not reaching their goals.

Those who have followed a misdirected path and want to change their route will find, like everything else that's worthwhile, that it isn't altogether easy. They have to have a determined will to change, and they might not be able to do it alone.

One of the best ways to become a better person is to involve yourself with people who are doing positive things. If you're in school, join clubs, involve yourself with sports. You will find that positive, young ambitious students are involved.

Sunday school and organized religious activities thrust you into a positive group. Get involved in some volunteer work if you have the spare time. Hospital, nursing home, playground supervision — these kinds of activities give you a sense of helping others. When you help others, you increase your own self-esteem.

Each day that a person improves himself puts him on a better road. It's easy to give up and accept your fate which could, if you allowed it, be very unwholesome and negative. Most people, if they really were honest with themselves, would prefer the positive route. Deciding that you are going to achieve is half the battle. The other half requires forward steps, consistently, without taking backward steps.

Persons cannot achieve their goals if they are chronic procrastinators. They must set the goals, work steadily toward them, eliminate the word "excuse" from their thoughts and vocabulary.

As you read this letter, you are going to find that I've included comments from other Black achievers. You also will find the names of Black heroes, past and present. These men have climbed the ladder to success. They have not followed the same occupations. They are from various college backgrounds and varied home settings. They also represent all sections of the country. The one thing that they have in common is that they are successful Black leaders. They are not all millionaires, but they all share their wealth in many ways, some with money, but all with the even more important gift of community involvement. Standing tall as role models, as examples, they are letting young Black men receive the inspiration and realization that "they too can do it."

You have the capability to determine your own fate, in your own hands. As you review the various steps which are necessary to achieve, and if you decide that success is your goal, then you must methodically follow the steps. You cannot jump over them and expect the same accomplishments of others who persevere. You also cannot expect to achieve successful goals on schedule if you take negative detours. You have a strong heritage. You have an obligation to yourself and to those who will follow you, to set goals and to make a difference. I urge you to do so.

All of us can improve. Those who have followed the steps and are moving along in positive ways toward their goals are to be commended. Some of you have found it easier than others. Some have had strong encouragement and your expectations have been consistently high. Others have been less fortunate. Role modeling has been limited. You, too, are to be commended for striving to break out of the mold.

Chapter 20
Hope

To quote the Bible, "Work! For the night cometh."

Henry Gates, Jr.
Professor and Writer
Harvard University

One of the main strengths of character that our early ancestors possessed was hope. As we look at the old Negro Spirituals and examine the titles, such songs as "Steal Away," "Nobody Knows the Trouble I've Seen," "Swing Low Sweet Chariot" all pointed toward hope. All through the Civil Rights movement, there was hope.

Much of what we witness today is something which only you can stop. The crime rate of Blacks has escalated. The tragedy of Black-on-Black crime is extreme. Killing each other reduces the Black male population and sends a large share of the remainder to penitentiaries. We are finding disproportionate numbers of Black women and children without adult male role models. Only you can turn the tide. If all young Black men would determine that they will make a difference, if each would assume personal responsibility to achieve positive goals, if each would realize how important it is that he make worthwhile contributions to society and become a positive role model, my efforts at writing this letter will have been greatly rewarded.

There are sources from which we develop our values. These include home, school, religious institutions, organizations, and our association with others. We adopt values we admire in others in these various settings. Sometimes young people develop very positive values which remain with them throughout their lives. Frequently young people adopt values which replace positive ones. Some of these "new" values are often acquired to pacify friends. But, values are not etched in stone. They do not have to remain permanent.

When people adopt negative values, and make mistakes in doing so, they can change. Those who do are helping themselves, and they also serve as models for others who have wanted to change their values, but needed a guide.

Each time a person pulls back to become a truly productive citizen, that's one less "problem" with which society must deal.

Persons who are productive, with a job, attending school or in training to qualify for particular positions, find themselves associating with other ambitious and positive people and have thereby increased their likelihood to reach their goals.

Chapter 21
Decision

Select a role model(s). Get an education. Believe in yourself and set goals for yourself. When choosing a mate, be sure that she shares your goals and ambitions.

Maurice Shirley
Director
Learning Opportunities Center
Milwaukee, Wisconsin

All men are different. I do not want to suggest that we all follow the same positive paths. I do want to suggest that no matter which path is followed, there are certain qualities which will be beneficial to young Black men. These include keeping goals in focus, and personal choices positive.

Young men will be tempted in various ways. They do not have to follow the crowd in order to have friends. Many young Black men think for themselves, and do not get mixed up with a group that ends up in trouble. Try associating with that positive group. You'll find that they're really okay. The young men who think for themselves are basically no different from the ones who follow the crowd. The difference is their aspiration to achieve. They stay on the steady study path. They realize that education opens many doors Many of them incidentally are competitors, athletes, musicians, debaters, or artists. They are anxious to see others join in with their group of aspiring young Black men.

All of you have every right to have high expectations and dream of bright futures. Let me remind you again with expectation, and with bright futures, steps must be taken. You cannot skip over steps and expect the same achievement as those who take each step in order.

Chapter 22
Faith and Decision Making

Very simply, the only way of assuring a productive life today is to get a good education. Anything else, like sports proficiency, quick financial fixes, are only temporary and can be gone in an instant. A good education is permanent, and is the basis for lasting growth.

Lynn Small
Account Supervisor
Equinox Add.

Young Black men will face many decisions throughout their life time. Let me assure you that decision-making is a process. Sometimes we make very quick, non-judgmental decisions, but we should always plan decisions.

There are several things to be considered. What is the outcome? How will this decision help? How will it hurt? Are there more advantages than disadvantages?

Young Black men's decisions will involve choices of friends, in-school activities, out-of-school activities. Choices will contribute toward their future. Positive things they do now will affect their status several years down the line.

Some non-achievers, ambitionless and negative, seem to attract others like a magnet and affect them in very negative ways. You must be determined not to let persons who have little desire for worthwhile things lead you around.

Young Black men have some unique challenges. During the last several decades, one of society's greatest downfalls has been a high incidence of illegal drug usage. Many young Black men have allowed themselves to succumb to the role of "middle men" — very few are top dealers but still illegally selling drugs. Some are lured into this lifestyle by money. Expensive cars and gold chains are incentives to pursue criminal activity. Patiently achieving these items through education and work will ensure an enduring lifestyle.

Everyone must have faith, a strong belief that accomplishment is attainable. Faith without effort or work is often futile. Don't think that you will reach goals through luck. Young Black men must believe in themselves and have a strong determination to reach for the goal. They cannot allow peer pressure to interfere.

Often friends don't realize the necessity of determined performance. They sometimes suggest opportunities for fun experiences which interfere with your set goals. Frequently young people are weak enough to give in to these pressures from some of their friends. When persons succumb to these pressures, they reduce their opportunities to reach their goals on schedule.

Chapter 23
Interviews with Outstanding Young Black Men

Prepare through education and wise handling of responsibility.

Jon R. Gray, Circuit Judge
16th Judicial Circuit of Missouri

David Johnson was the head basketball coach of Hickman High School, Columbia, Missouri. This was special for David. This is the high school from which David graduated just ten years earlier.

David grew up in a loving environment with his parents and five brothers and sisters. His father early instilled a feeling in him for what it takes to be a man. After his senior year in high school he decided to reach for more than being on the streets. "You have to break away and realize that there's something else," he says.

Johnson left home to attend a junior college in Minnesota. He says it was quite a culture shock. He worked hard to make things happen and to blend his experiences with those he discovered there. Johnson's main focus was education. Basketball was a tool, but education was more important.

David's junior college coach compared the game of basketball with the game of life. David never met Dr. Julius Erving, but Erving's achievements on and off the courts inspired him. Johnson referred to Erving as a great ambassador. His college experiences were positive.

David's father was his special role model. As a teenager he said he stood and listened to lectures from his father. Sometimes he didn't want to, but the lectures gave him a feeling of dignity and respect.

David's heroes are Black leaders and what they represent. He looks at professional athletes with different eyes, but he admires most "those who are everyday people, who rear their families and make progress."

David's advice to young Black men today is, "Set goals and, regardless if scared or not, achieve them. You can overcome the fears of lack of succeeding. Also, achieve educationally at the highest possible level that you can."

When asked why some young Black men achieve, yet others of similar background seem to care little about themselves or their future, he said, "It goes back to fear of not succeeding. Rather than try, they give up and tend to want to run around them. They get in a rut and have no place to go. They grow up in a society where this attitude is the norm, and they don't know how to get out of it."

When asked about his most positive qualities, David answered, "I listen to feelings that others express. I'm genuine. I really care for people."

His long range goals are to complete a doctorate and eventually become an athletic director high school, college or professional. He listed his major reason for achievement as a strong desire to be successful, to be able to provide adequately for his family, and to be happy doing in is work.

David's response to the role which he can play in helping young men to achieve was, "With my experience and knowledge, I hope to be able to pass on to young men the feeling that if they really want to make it, they can. There's no short cut to success. You must work hard at it. It will pay off."

Benjamin Ezekwe was born in Nigeria, a member of a family of twelve. His early schooling was in Nigeria and Liberia. He has received a bachelor's degree from Lincoln University in Jefferson City, Missouri, completed additional course work at Columbia College of Columbia, Missouri, and is currently enrolled in the college of pharmacy at Drake University.

Benjamin states his positive experiences. "Home was a place of happiness." Both parents were very supportive with school and church. He was a member of the church choir and an active participant in mass with the Catholic church. He learned respect for others, and commented, "If you don't respect others, you won't receive respect." This was a philosophy he received from his father.

Another view which he holds is, "If you're attempting to do something, aim for the highest goal." Another thing that he learned early and recited frequently in grade school was:

> Try, try, try again.
> If you try and don't succeed,
> Try, try again.
> Then your courage should appear,

For if you will persevere
Then you should conquer, never fear.
Try, try, try again.

When asked about major role models as a youth, he replied, "My father. People looked up to him. People with money and a lot of material things came to my father for advice." Benjamin wants to be like his father, except to achieve higher.

When asked about current heroes, he stated, "Martin Luther King, Malcolm X, Jesse Jackson and Mandela."

What advice do you offer young Black men today? His reply:

1. Stay in school.
2. Never settle for the minimum.
3. Remember, Rome wasn't built in a day. If you want a cookie, you have to work for it.
4. Follow your mind. Don't follow the crowd. Do what you know are the right things.
5. You can be anything you want to be in this country.

When asked why some young Black men are achievers and others of similar background care little about themselves and their future, his responses were, "It starts from family and family values, and some don't have good positive examples. They make bad choices so often that they think it's too late to change."

When asked about his own most positive qualities, his response was, "I am determined. When I decide to do something, I will not stop until my goal has been achieved. My goal is primary. Any possible interference is secondary. I look at myself and say to myself, I can do anything anyone else can do. Nothing's impossible. If Dick can do it, or Harry can do it, I can too."

What are your long range goals? "My goals are to become a pharmacist and to manage a corporation. I want to help young Black men to realize that they can accomplish positive goals."

What do you consider to be the major reasons for your determination to achieve? "I like good things, to be able to own a house and be like the people I look up to. I have to go to school and prepare myself."

"I told my parents that one day I'm going to be a doctor, pharmacist or veterinarian. I want to fulfill my promise."

"My friends are a big influence. Some are doing doctoral work. A cousin is a medical student in Iowa. A cousin in Massachusetts is a civil engineer. I look at them and realize that I too have what it takes."

Chapter 24
Your Obligation as a Young Black Man

> My message to young Black males is based on the following values:
> I. Education, Education, Education
> II,. Develop a concept of who you are. Know yourself.
> III. Love yourself and others.
> IV. Respect yourself; respect the rights/property of others.
> V. Decide what you want to be. Set goals for yourself. Help people to understand who you are.
> VI. Develop a plan for yourself and work the plan.
>
> Vernon V. Gavin
Educator

If young Black men shirk their responsibility and, while others move forward, they step backward or even remain in the same spot, they are reducing the level of accomplishment of Black men.

As we look around, we see many Black men in powerful positions. Black men are involved in the national government. They are state leaders, they are mayors of cities, they are superintendents of schools, they are church leaders, they are business owners, and on corporate boards of directors, they are hospital administrators, researchers, they have sharp legal minds.

Then we blink and look in another direction. Black men are prisoners, they are on drugs, they are pimps, they are in gangs, they are unemployed.

We look again and we see many Black men who are working hard to support their families. They are mechanics and bus drivers, they work in hotels and restaurants, they drive taxis, are orderlies, servicemen. They are honest, hard-working citizens who are men in the middle. All of you do not have to climb to the top level. Honest, hard-working men in the middle are a group of men who deserve admiration.

The other group so many young men gravitate toward is the group which I implore young Black men to avoid, the group which lives from day to day without goals.

Young Black men have many opportunities in life to make choices. If they have made unwise choices, and most of us have, it isn't too late to change. Young men owe it to themselves and to the future of total society to climb up and out from negative behavior.

All of us have on occasion succumbed to peer pressure. Peer pressure is good if it is positive. If we are getting encouragement from others to do something that is positive, that's super. On the other hand, negative peer pressure seems to rear its ugly head all too frequently. We know when we are encouraged to do wrong. We also are aware that many of the negative activities in which our peers encourage us to engage could lead to real trouble. Somehow, we don't seem to care. We give in to the pressure and the real problems start.

Statistics show us that young Black men are in prisons and jails nationwide in excessive numbers. Many of the men who are there are incarcerated because of having succumbed to peer pressure. Many are really not "hardened criminals." They are victims of following the crowd.

Everyone must be his own person. He must set his own standards, have positive values, set goals and work steadily toward them. As we look around and see the Black men who have achieved, let me assure you they were not born with any advantages. It isn't easy, but it's worth the effort to take the necessary steps to become successful.

We have seen the T-shirts worn by many Blacks with the words "Black Power." We have watched Black men Olympic winners as they are giving the Black power sign.

Young Black men have much power. Most of the power that they possess is personal power. They have the power to direct themselves and to accomplish their goals. They have the power to be ambitious or to be lazy.

They have the power to be leaders or followers. They have the power to climb or to fall. They have the power to study and learn or to waste time and fail. They have the power to misuse their power, or to use it well.

During recent years we have witnessed the pride of American Blacks who have chosen to don dredlocks and to wear clothing of Africa. African art has become more popular for African-Americans recently. It is inspiring to see the attachment which Blacks have placed upon their African heritage. This outward display of strong feeling toward our African heritage should also require a realization of what it is that we are depicting. Our African heritage points us to a people who were and are proud.

Today as we look at the typical athlete from Africa and at his stature, he stands with pride, he looks statuesque. He is a winner before he begins to run. As we look at and listen to the leaders of various African nations, we see pride, we see winners. When we look at the symmetry, and think of the skills of those who built the pyramids of Egypt, we again are filled with pride.

As we decide to wear African dress or wear an African hairstyle, think of its meaning. The word "pride" immediately comes to mind. If there is pride, then we must also acquire stature, we must look men in the eye, we must become even more determined to achieve.

What do I say to young men? You have a strong heritage. You have a reason to hold your head up and to be proud. You will profit greatly in proportion to your determination to improve yourself. You can be a leader. You don't have to be a follower. Positive behavior is necessary to achieve positive goals. Negative behavior leads to negative results. The jails and prisons are filled with those who commit crimes against society. There are positive routes which we all can take. This answer to accomplishment is the same as it was 50 years ago when I was a teenager.

Chapter 25
Interviews with Incarcerated Young Black Men

> You have to work harder to stay even with society. Even though things often don't come out even, you still have to do what you think is right and live by your decision.
>
> Phil Bradley, Formerly Head Baseball Coach
> Westminster College
> Fulton, Missouri

There are several ways that persons climb the ladder toward successful goals. You take each step carefully. Usually when a person is attempting to climb, those on the upper rungs reach down and give assistance.

One of the most important phases of climbing the ladder is a determination to reach the goal. There seems to be a person or a group of persons who are themselves not ambitious. This group frequently makes attempts to pull down the climber. You must be determined not to allow others to cause you to lose sight of the prize. Those who attempt to cause you not to achieve usually are themselves non-achievers, and they usually years later regret that they have limited their opportunities, and greatly reduced their income potential.

Young Black men must show that they are strong and that they will not give in to negative behavior. There are those who look up to the wrong models. Just imagine that you're in a shop class and everyone's been given a pattern of a birdhouse to build. Somehow, you were given by mistake, a pattern of a magazine rack. Either you call the error to the attention of your teacher, or you build the wrong item.

The same process is true of your role models. If, mistakenly, you select a drug pusher as your model, you are going to either change your negative model, or you will develop negative behavior.

Many young men who are in prison are really basically good people. Some have had few opportunities in life, however all have had choices. It isn't easy to break the cycle. It requires a very determined, strong-willed person not to follow the crowd or the bad examples. I am aware that crime is very common in many neighborhoods. I am also aware that some young men, from those same neighborhoods, thrive and achieve in very positive and productive ways. When we look at the jails and prisons in our country and see the disproportionate number of Black men behind bars, it's disheartening. When we also look at the reasons that Black men are incarcerated, we note that many are drug-related in some way. There is no doubt that Black men are capable of high achievement. As I met and talked with several young Black men in prison, I was amazed to realize how intelligent many of them were. It was sad that all of this talent within a race of people is being locked up. What we are doing to ourselves by involving ourselves in major criminal activity is deplorable.

The following is a letter I received from a prisoner.

Mr. Battle,

...I hope this letter finds you in the best of health and spirits. Mr. Battle, I want to thank you for allowing me the opportunity to tell my side of the story and just listen to what I have to say. I enclosed a visiting form, please return that as soon as possible. It is difficult for me to conceive of any other situation which places greater hardship and depression on one's mind and soul than the predicament I find myself in today. "Prison" has been rough but it deepened my emotions. It's made me think about life, and it's pushed me toward independence. After being locked up almost ten months in the Department of Corrections, I'm here to tell you that the problems of crime and violence and the terror, fear and insecurity they produce in our lives, our homes, our community are real. Many of our children are in trouble. And I really do mean our children, and they are in trouble across racial lines. I'm speaking a lot about Black children, particularly the plight of young African-American males, because many of them seem to be in the most desperate and despairing situations. A Black child born today has only a one in five chance of growing up with the two parents until the age of sixteen. Also, one out of four Black males in the world today is under some kind of supervision (probation/ parole: federal, state). The statistics are horrifying. I often wonder how many of us bother to even think about, let alone question, the assumption

that young Black kids in trouble are not problem kids in need of help, but bad kids that need to be disposed of. Gary Graham's case, like so many others, represents a growing pattern on the part of the justice system to criminalize Black youth. My situation at present seems at (this) time uncertain, if not perilous, but I will never wither in despair and cease to struggle for my freedom. After practically ten months of being confined in this house of horrors, I still haven't grown accustomed to living here. I hope that I never will. I still have hope and high expectations of surviving this raging storm of injustice and regaining my freedom someday. I ask that you continue to share in this hope with me.... It is my hope that when I am released from confinement that I will be able to speak and tell my story to young children, for that matter, whoever will listen and wants to learn how and what to do to stay out of the web of the Department of Corrections. I look forward to seeing you soon. And please give your wife my respects.

Respectfully and sincerely,
Name Withheld

Another prisoner, Tony is 22, married and father of two children. Tony grew up in a large urban city. His parents were together when he was very young but separated before he was five. His idol was his paternal grandfather, but he died when Tony was about ten. He has an older brother and a younger brother and sister. During his early years, Tony was a student, played football and boxed while in junior high. He got into trouble when he was thirteen for stealing. He stated that at home he had very little, and that he reached the age when he wanted to have several changes of clothing, so he was caught stealing some. He was released to his mother and he stated that he felt that he had learned his lesson.

Tony lived in a drug-infested neighborhood during his pre-teen and early teen years. He said although he drank, he stayed away from drugs because he didn't want to be like those he saw who were hooked on them. His neighbors, he stated, even "shot up drugs" in front of little children, five to six years old. He felt that was a terrible thing to do, and he stayed away from them.

He began running around with a crowd that stayed out all night riding around drinking and partying. "Life didn't have a real meaning for me," he said.

Although Tony expressed that he himself tried to do right, he went through a phase that could only lead to trouble. He spoke highly of his boxing coach, whom he felt tried to serve as a model for him and treated him like a family member.

Tony became involved with a young lady who became pregnant when he was eighteen years old. He married her, moved into an apartment, got a job as a chauffeur and felt that things finally were looking up. The apartment was in a little better neighborhood, but still one in which drug sales and use were common.

Tony stated that late one evening there was a knock at his door when his wife and year-old son were at home. He answered the door and the man there, whom he had never seen, demanded drugs. He stated that he told him he didn't have anything and then words ensued. They yelled at each other before Tony got his gun and shot the man who died later in the evening at the hospital.

Tony stated that he continued to work and tried to live in a "good way." About eight months after the incident, he was picked up by the police, and has now been prison for a year. He says his mother, his wife and children make weekly visits to see him.

Tony is a convicted criminal. In talking with him, I found him to be a very intelligent young man. He dropped out of school at eighteen and since his incarceration, has passed the GED and continues to take college courses in prison. He wants to get a business degree and combine his training to include preparation for work as a computer analyst.

When asked about early role models, he said, "Tony Dorsett and mostly the Lakers." When he became older his role models were Martin Luther King and Malcolm X. He feels that in order to show the race how to get out of problems, it's not a "single" battle, really more of a "group" battle.

When asked what advice he has for young Black men, his comment was, "Tell them we all make mistakes, but we have to recognize the mistakes in order to change them. Also, don't give up. Stay away from those things out there (drugs, late hours, low life, etc.). You don't need them. Don't join the pack, stay on the outside of it so you can walk away.

"Society must realize that we all make mistakes. Society then must help us and reward us for our accomplishments." His other advice was, "Unity can be found in your neighborhood, if you give yourself a chance to really know each other."

As you read this letter and read the suggestions made by all of the Black men to you as young Black men, there is one thread that goes through all. Don't quit. Get an education.

There are represented among the men educators, attorneys, physicians, pharmacists, business men, governors, mayors and several men who are incarcerated. They all responded to the question, what advice do you offer to young Black men? I urge you to occasionally review their responses and use them as guidelines for your conduct in the future.

As I visited one of the prisons and talked with inmates, one of the questions I invariably asked was, "What are your plans when you are released?"

The most common response, even from the men committed for murder was, "To help in some way in the Black community." I know that all men who responded in this manner, likely when released, will not be involved in the positive activities that they describe. I know, however, some will. If these jailed prisoners even voice these positive plans, what about you? Some of you have gotten into some hassles with legal authorities, but that doesn't mean you can't make a positive turnaround.

All of us have made some mistakes. The test of a real man is how he reacts after the mistake has been made. If instead of continued negative behavior, a person pulls around and climbs up and out of the problems, then he's on a good road.

Always remember that positive goals are attainable. Never give up.

Andrew Dowe
Computer Specialist
Boston, MA

WEAPONS FISTS, KNIVES AND PISTOLS

One of the most enjoyable pastimes for young people during pre-television period was going to the movies and viewing cowboy pictures, commonly called "shoot-em-ups." These were generally predictable — the good guys versus the bad, and invariably the good guys won.

Somehow, it seems that a favorite pastime of many young Black men now is the practice of "shoot-em-up." Not really the good guy versus the bad guy, but instead "Black-on-Black" killing. Somehow, it seems that fighting and the use of knives and guns by many Black men is a pastime. The cowboy pictures of the past were largely fictional reenactments of the settling of the West. The current practices of the many youth who involve themselves in negative behavior sometimes involves group or gang activity. The result culminates in serious injury or actual killing, and this is followed by one more "inmate" housed in a state penitentiary. This is a bleak scenario, but it is a serious activity and a dramatic threat to a society.

Black-on-Black crime is a relatively new activity. Booker T. Washington, the founder of Tuskegee Institute in 1881 and author of *Up From Slavery*, stated "I shall not let any man drag me so low as to make me hate him."

When we look at the latter part of the 19th century and the early years of the 20th century, we witness the founding of many Black colleges. Black men had great aspirations and many made upward climbs. Now we, one hundred years later, can look with pride over many of the accomplishments which have taken place. But a dark cloud hangs over us which causes grief. Black crime. If you will direct all of your energies toward positive achievement and work toward improvement, think of what a difference you can all make in the 21st century.

Chapter 26
Conclusion: A Personal Challenge to Young Black Men

You can all improve. You must all realize that worthwhile accomplishments require time, planning, determination, hard work, and the acceptance of disappointments. You will find that you cannot predict who in your neighborhood will reach positive goals. Sometimes the ones who work slowly but consistently by-pass some who seem to have greater ability.

If you look through your high school yearbook, you see pictures of schoolmates who have potential but who, for whatever the reason, don't make it. You see others who, although possibly not the top achievers, were persistent and stayed away from trouble, and they achieved.

I challenge you, if you are a student, to make proper use of your time as you prepare your assignments and review for various tests. I challenge you to look upon school as an important stepping stone to your personal success. I challenge you to realize that achievement is not the result of an accident, but it is accomplished by way of a road map.

I challenge you to hold your head high with respect and to look any man directly in the eyes.

I challenge you to be a goal setter and then a pace setter.

I challenge you to show respect to your parents and teachers. By doing this, you are showing self-respect.

I give you the same challenge that Dr. Mary McLeod Bethune gave to Black youth throughout the country, "Young folks, do something. Be somebody."

You do not really have a choice of which route you should follow. You really have an ultimatum. You owe a great debt to past fighters for rights.

If you take a negative position, you are a traitor to the cause for racial improvement. Your individual family deserves proper conduct from you. Your individual neighborhoods and communities likewise deserve that each of its residents do his part to improve the community, not destroy it. You owe it to yourself to achieve to your highest possible level.

I'm sure that many of you share with me feelings of sorrow and remorse when you see the many young men of our country who show a "don't care" attitude and who exhibit very negative postures and conduct, foul language, fighting, thievery, car jacking, knifing, drive-by shooting and overt killing. All are activities which contribute to the stereotypical images unfairly causing others to think this is normal, typical, expected behavior of young Black men. Of course, just as with most negative activity, these kinds of conduct make newspaper headlines and lead stories on television news.

There are many young Black men who are far from the stereotypical description. These rarely make headlines or television reports, but they are there in great numbers. It is my fervent hope that many others of you will realize that the best route to success takes time, the best route produces lasting happiness, and the best route also contributes toward the debt that we all owe to Black men of the past. I have no doubt that all of you can make a positive contribution. I challenge you to do it.

If you are parents, teachers or are just interested in improving the plight of our young men, I sincerely thank you and hope that this writing will assist you. I also admonish you to never give up. [5]